# Dublin's Little Jerusalem

# Dublin's Little Jerusalem

Nick Harris

A. & A. Farmar

British Library cataloguing in Publication Data
A CIP catalogue record for this book is available from the
British Library.


Cover design by Alice Campbell
Cover illustration 'Merchants' Hill, Winetavern Street' by Harry Kernoff
Text edited, designed and set by A. & A. Farmar
Printed and bound by GraphyCems

ISBN 1-899047-90-5

First published in 2002
by
A. & A. Farmar
Beech House
78 Ranelagh Village
Dublin 6
Ireland
Tel: 353 1 496 3625
Fax: 353 1 497 0107
Email: afarmar@iol.ie
Web: farmarbooks.com

# Contents

*This book is dedicated to my dear wife Riv,
our daughter Valerie
and our granddaughters
Dalia and Tasha*

# Foreword

My parents never spoke about their life in Russia when they were young. They never even mentioned their own parents and I never knew of any aunts or uncles, except for my father's brother who went to America. I wish I had known more about them. I hope that my daughter and granddaughters will not be saying the same thing about me in the years to come. This is why I set out to share some memories of the family into which I was born in 1915 and over eighty-six years of my life in the Dublin Jewish community.

I was fortunate to witness a community grow up in Dublin to maturity where it seemed that the whole population were involved in some way or another in communal activities. Our community life centred around one small street known as 'Little Jerusalem'—Clanbrassil Street.

The Jewish Community in the best years never reached more than five and a half thousand persons. A noticeable increase came during the end of the 1930s when Jewish people came from Britain to escape the pending war with Germany. A small number of refugees also came who had managed to escape the anti-Semitism that flared up in Europe. Unfortunately, too many countries, including Ireland, refused sanctuary to many others who later perished. A general decline in numbers took place from 1950 onwards when the young people, especially girls, including our own daughter, decided that they wanted a better way of life and emigrated to England and other countries.

While the immigrant men brought with them a rich culture and knowledge of *Yiddishkeit*, it was the women who brought the customs and traditions they had been raised with, and it was the women who were responsible for setting up a *kosher* home with meagre possessions and the onerous task of feeding the family.

I am not a historian and my book does not claim to be a historical record. Some of the events and some of the people I write about may be remembered differently by others. Each person has their own memories of growing up in Dublin and my aim is to ignite and rekindle those memories, and if I can succeed in this I will have achieved my purpose in writing this book.

I hope my endeavours in this book will help people to visualise the kind of fortitude and sacrifices that our parents made to give us a better life than their own. We should be eternally grateful to them.

I am grateful to the many people who offered additional information about their families and activities; to Elizabeth Lovatt Dolan, my editor, whose guidance and help was of enormous benefit in writing this book; to Raphael Siev, Curator of the Irish Jewish Museum, for his invaluable assistance; to Howard Freeman and Carol Bolger for their help in typing the manuscript; and to my next-door-neighbour Pat McHenry, who computerised my drawing of the street map of the area where most of the Dublin Jewish community lived and did their shopping. Above all, I am grateful to my very good friend Joe Briscoe without whose encouragement I would never have undertaken this project.

*Nick Harris*
*April 2002*

# 1 Russian Roots

My parents, Israel Bernard and Edith Chachanoff, arrived in Dublin in the early 1900s. They came from a small Lithuanian town called Dobny Myser Mokilve. Shortly after their marriage they decided to leave Russia. If they had stayed my father would have been conscripted into the Tsar's army. They left Russia thinking that they were going to America. My father's brother had already emigrated and he sent the money to pay for their passage to America. In actual fact my parents, like thousands of other Jews fleeing from Russia, were dumped in England or Ireland by the captain of the ship. When my parents first set foot in England, they thought they were in America. It did not take them too long to realise that they were in a different country, but by then there was nothing they could do about it.

When they presented their papers to an Aliens Officer on arrival in England, he asked my father his name. My father replied 'Chachanoff' and then he was asked to spell it. The officer was unable to spell the Russian name and my father could not spell it in English. The officer proposed to put the name down as Cohen, but my father showed him a piece of paper with the name Harris that his brother Sam had taken when he got to America. This is how we got the name Harris. No doubt, many Jewish people who left Russia and Poland—and also some of the Irish who went to America—around that time would have had a similar experience.

The one thing my father had when he arrived in England, and later in Ireland, was a trade. He had exceptional talent as a tailor and must have had excellent training in a large tailoring establishment near his home town. He would have been termed a Master Tailor, able to cut his own patterns for any style and size. I know he brought the patterns with him when he eventually came to Dublin. Being a tailor, he must have got a job very quickly in England. As far as I have been able to work out, he and my mother settled in Birmingham for a number of years. I have discovered that they also lived in Wolverhampton and later, for some reason that I never knew, they went to live and work in the Isle of Man. There must have been a Jewish community there at that time. They appear to have been in England for over six years and must have saved some money before coming to Ireland. Three of their eight children, Leah, Sam and Hymie, were born before they moved to Dublin. Harry, Nathan (myself), Jean, Louis and Sadie were born in Dublin.

Sometimes when I am lying in bed at night, unable to sleep, I think about how my parents and other Jewish people left the place where they were born and left their parents, their brothers, sisters and friends, to seek a new life in faraway countries that they had only heard of. It seems that Sam, my father's brother, who had managed to get to America, sent letters to his parents describing the opportunities in America and urging my father and mother to follow him there. I have a photo of my uncle Sam and his wife. They adopted a boy and a girl. Sadly we never met them.

I can imagine the anguish when they decided to emigrate and to leave the homes of their youth, knowing in their hearts that they would never see their parents and friends again. I never met my uncle in America, but from piecing together certain bits of information I think that he must have sent my parents money to pay for their travel costs. I know nothing about this chapter of their early life or about their journey to what they assumed would be America. They must have been incredibly brave and very apprehensive as they set out with few possessions but with a determination to succeed.

Most of the Jews who came to Ireland in the early 1900s had very little money and could not speak English. When I was growing up I had the impression that my father was not a very forceful character. Later on, I came to the conclusion that this was because he couldn't express his feelings adequately as he did not have a sufficient command of the English language. When he left Russia, taking his young wife into the unknown, he could only have spoken Russian and Yiddish.

Having some knowledge of English after his years in England, he was able to find work quickly in Dublin. He got a position in a small clothing factory owned by Morris Ellis in Middle Abbey Street. Mr Ellis's main customers were sailors from ships that docked at the North Wall. My father was quickly put in charge of the workroom and he stayed with Mr Ellis until he had sufficient money to start his own tailoring business. He rented two rooms in Aungier Street, called the firm the XL Tailors, and employed a tailoress called Mrs McCarthy. I got to know Mrs McCarthy during the school holidays when my mother used to send me to his workrooms with my father's lunch.

From that beginning in Aungier Street, my father went on to much larger premises at 8 Lower Ormond Quay, employing over twenty people. These included three Jewish men: two were machiners and the third was a presser. At that time it was not unusual for men to be using sewing machines. In later years it was mainly women who were employed as machinists. The next move was to Smithfield where he started a factory employing fifty to sixty people in the early 1930s. Finally, in 1935, he moved to a factory of over 8,000 square feet in Capel Street, employing over 100 people. His own expertise was the most important factor in this development, and he expected his children to play their part in the growth of the business that would be theirs one day.

My father worked very hard. He never gambled and he never drank, except on Friday night when he would have a small glass of wine after he had said the *Kiddush** (the prayer that sanctifies the Sabbath) and allowed us to taste the wine. Before he left for work in the morning he always had a coal fire going and brought a hot drink to my mother in bed. Our parents were good parents. They were always there for us. We were never short of food or clothing and we were a very healthy family. When I think of my mother coming to Dublin with three young children and then having five more, she obviously had her hands full. But great credit must be given to her for rearing and feeding such a large family.

Our parents' only concern was to provide for their family. I never heard either of them complaining about their early years. They never spoke about their own childhood, and they never spoke about the hardships they must have suffered to make it possible for us, their children, to have the lifestyle we now enjoy. They had little time for holidays. I do, however, remember a day when I was very young and a letter came to Greenville Terrace from the Isle of Man inviting my father and mother to visit the Hyman family there. The Hymans had befriended my parents when they were living in the Isle of Man, and must have kept in touch after they came to Dublin. My sister Sadie remembers that both our parents once went to Scarborough, but I have no recollection of that trip.

I overheard my mother saying they couldn't go—she had to look after the family and my father could not leave his business. But mother was persuaded to go by Mr and Mrs Eppel, who lived two doors away from our house. Finally, she went for one week. My eldest sister Leah and my little sister Sadie went with her. When the three of them returned, we heard that the crossing to the Isle of Man had been very rough and my mother thought she was going to die. But she recovered quickly and they had a lovely week with the Hymans. The return journey was very pleasant and the holiday was a talking point for a long time afterwards. Mrs Eppel had promised

* *A glossary of Yiddish terms begins on page 217.*

to look after the rest of us. She cooked for all of us, and I can recall my brother Harry, myself, and my sister Jean going to the Eppels' house for meals. I also recall Mr Eppel's flowing white beard.

I can never remember my father scolding me, or for that matter encouraging me in any way. I never remember him taking us for a walk or telling stories. But I do remember the time my mother took a few of us to see Al Jolson in one of the first talking pictures. I also remember her taking us on a charabanc (today it would be referred to as a coach) to the mountains where we had a picnic. My parents were not at all demonstrative. I never experienced either parent giving me a hug, and I never heard any endearments. Looking back, I have no doubt that we were loved. It was just not expressed as it would be by parents today. We had wonderful caring parents whom we can be proud of, and I know that these sentiments are shared by nearly all those whose parents came to Dublin and made such a contribution to our city. There is a similarity between the experience of the Jews of Dublin and the millions of Irish people who, forced by circumstances, had to leave their homes during the famine years of the 1840s. They travelled as poor emigrants and succeeded beyond belief in making good in America.

Like many other children at the time, when I and my brothers and sisters were growing up we were left to our own resources. We may have been high spirited and mischievous, but we knew right from wrong. We were always well behaved and we were brought up to be helpful to elderly people, whether they were Jewish or non-Jewish. This was instilled in us by our mother who was the dominant person in our home. She would nearly always know where we were going. If we were told to be home at a certain time we knew we would get a clip on the ear if we were late. Naturally, there was more latitude as we grew older. We used to refer to our parents as 'old-fashioned', but at that time we were too young to understand the conditions they were brought up in. Now our own children tell us that we ourselves are 'old-fashioned'. Of the eight children, three of us are left: Louis, Sadie and myself. Louis now lives in Devon, and Sadie lives in Manchester.

When my mother died in March 1948, Louis was the only one still living at home in Dufferin Avenue. After my mother's death my father received many visits from his very religious friends. Louis heard some of them saying it was not right that a widower should be on his own and he should think of getting married again. As his children, we knew that he was lonely, and he was not the kind of man who wanted to visit his sons' homes. He was never comfortable in company. I can recall being in my brother Sam's home when he was there for a meal. He hardly spoke unless somebody asked him a direct question. Several months after our mother died, we were quite shocked when we heard that he had remarried.

Louis noticed that people were coming to the house, but he was not aware of what they were talking about. He remembers Louis Steinberg calling for father one day and the two of them going out, with father carrying a small suitcase, but not a word as to where they were going. About a week later they arrived back with this strange woman. Father said nothing to Louis as to who the woman was, but Louis Steinberg introduced her to him as his father's wife. Louis told me that father never suggested that he should stay on in the house, or even talked about his new wife or where she came from. Louis was dumbfounded and at a loss what to do, but having nowhere else to go he had no option but to stay where he was. Just at that time, May 1948, there was a call for volunteers to go to Israel as the United Nations had voted in favour of Israel having its own state. Israel was attacked by the Arab countries, and appealed for help to Jewish boys and girls to come to Israel. Asher Benson was acting for the Jewish Agency in Dublin, enlisting Jewish boys and girls for the army and offering them free passage to Israel. Louis volunteered immediately, and served for about two years.

He remembers going to London with Abe Garb, a son of the *chazan* (cantor). They went from London to Paris and then on a very crowded train to Marseilles where they boarded a ship for Haifa. The ship was packed not only with young people going to fight, but also with old men and women wanting to get out of Europe. Louis lay down on the deck, as the heat below was stifling. Because he was very fair and was lying in the full glare of the sun, he suffered sunstroke and needed attention from one of the doctors on board the ship. So he had unpleasant memories of the journey.

Three days later, when they had reached Haifa, he was brought to a kibbutz. During this time he got separated from Abe Garb and never saw him again. He was attached to the 72nd battalion, B Company, and given a rifle and some ammunition. After a few hours practice he was allocated to a trench protected by sand bags. He was not involved in any action at this point, but remembers an incident when he was defending another kibbutz. It was during the night, and he heard bullets hitting the sand bags. They heard the 'phut phut' sound and just fired back blindly.

He was then put in charge of a machine gun called a 'Besa', which he said came from Czechoslovakia. A target was put up during a practice drill with the machine gun. He won the competition for accuracy. On duty one day, he thought that the sights on the machine gun were not correct, so he had to make the necessary adjustment. If he had not done so, he would have been firing at a trench where some Americans were on guard. He said that everything was hit and miss at the time. On a day when there was very little activity, he decided to walk across a field to another trench. On the way back he took a different route. When he was half way across the field, he noticed that members of his battalion were waving and shouting. When he arrived safely the officer in charge shouted at him 'You bloody mad Irishman, do you realise you have just walked over a minefield.' Louis felt very sheepish about this.

One day, when they had moved to another kibbutz, he was with an American when they came across a young Arab girl and a little boy. The American said 'Let's shoot the bastards.' Louis thought he was joking. But the American was serious. He started to undo the catch on his rifle, saying that they deserved to be killed. Then Louis said to him 'Put the catch back again; you're not doing any shooting. Can't you see they are only youngsters out for a walk.' With some reluctance, the American put the catch back and nobody was hurt.

Gradually, the fighting stopped, but the battalion was still on duty and they passed the time playing football with the oranges that were lying on the ground. They were never short of food—no meat but plenty of eggs, chicken and dairy foods. A few weeks later they were told that the war was over. The volunteers were discharged and Louis received a gratuity, less a sum of money for the loss of a helmet that he had given away. They were left to their own devices, but were allowed to stay in the kibbutz.

Louis became friendly with two South Africans. They were volunteers like himself. They asked him to stay on in Israel with them, as they were planning to start a delivery service bringing food and other goods from one town to another. He was very tempted to go into business with them, but felt that he would not be able to take the extreme heat and decided to return to Dublin.

He enjoyed the return journey. The ship to Marseilles was nearly empty and he was free to wander around the deck. But when he was on the boat from Holyhead to Dublin he began to worry. He felt that he would not be welcome in the house with his new stepmother, so he got in touch with our brother Hymie. Hymie and his wife Ruby agreed that Louis could live with them, and he stayed there for many years before moving to London.

While Louis was away I had not actually met my stepmother. I did see her with my father once or twice. Hymie told me that her name was Malvern. He also told me that she was a survivor from a concentration camp, but never talked about her experience in the camp and never wanted to talk about it. Hymie thought that she had been married before and that her husband had died in the camps, but he did not know if she had children. I asked him what she was like, as I intended going to the house on the Sunday. Hymie found it difficult to form an opinion about her, but said that he and Ruby thought she was a nice person and seemed very intelligent.

I decided to form my own opinion, and took my children to Dufferin Avenue one Sunday morning. I knocked on the door. My father opened it and stood there looking at us. For a moment I thought we were not going to be asked in. The first thing I noticed in the front room was that the chesterfield suite was covered with white sheets. My stepmother came in. My father never introduced me to her, so I just said Hello and introduced the children. The atmosphere was very strained. The children were offered biscuits but I don't remember if I was offered anything. We stayed for a short time and then left. At least the ice was broken.

When I started going to Greenville Hall *shul* (synagogue) on Saturdays, I always sat beside my father. But he never suggested that I go back to his house for a cup of coffee or a drink. One *Shabbos* (Sabbath) I said I would like to see Malvern and we walked back together to the house which was only around the corner. I was offered a glass of *Kiddush* wine. I found it very difficult to make conversation, but I was determined to keep going to the house after *shul* occasionally.

Eventually, I felt that my father had done the right thing in remarrying—but not in such haste, even though I was aware that he was talked into it. He needed to be with a companion. At least, he was looked after. You might ask why we did not invite him and Malvern to our home. The only ones they visited were Sam and Hetty, and Hymie and Ruby once or twice. They never invited any of us to Dufferin Avenue.

When my father died in August 1966, Malvern was left quite comfortable. She had the house and an income. I used to take her out for drives with Riv and my mother-in-law. One day she remarked to my mother-in-law that when children get married the parents are no longer responsible for them. I thought that was a strange thing to say, but it suggested to me that she never had any children of her own. I was very surprised when I learned that Malvern had a sister living in Dublin. Her name was Brand. She had been in Dublin since around 1930. I realised that I knew her husband. His first name was Herman and he came to Ireland from Czechoslovakia around 1925. He was an engineer and he came over when the Irish Glass Bottle Company was being set up in Ringsend. He often came to our home, but I think his wife came to Dublin later. He used to play cards with my brother-in-law, Sam Farbenbloom, who was from the same town in Czechoslovakia.

After some time, Malvern sold the house in Dufferin Avenue and went to live with her sister. A year or so later, I was surprised to hear that she had died. I went to her funeral and recited the *Kaddish* (mourners' prayer). Then I said prayers for her for a month. Not long afterwards, I saw her sister in the Jewish Home. Having nobody in the house with her after Malvern died, she had decided to live in the Home. I had a long conversation with her—much longer than I ever had with Malvern.

A week or so later, I got a message that Mrs Brand wanted to see me. When I arrived at the Home, she asked me up to her room and handed me a portrait of my father, saying that it had been painted in Italy and Malvern wanted me to have it. She told me that Malvern always liked me, and had said that my father was very happy whenever I was called up to recite the *Haftorah* (a passage from the Prophets). I often wonder if my father was happy that he had married Malvern. I know he was a good husband to my mother and I have no doubt that he looked after Malvern. I also remember that Malvern told me many times that my father was a good kind man.

# 2 Childhood in Little Jerusalem

I was born in Dublin in 1915 at 14 Greenville Terrace, off the South Circular Road. When I was applying for a passport around 1946, I needed a birth certificate. When I got the certificate I noticed that the date of my birth was given as 26 June 1915. But I had always celebrated my birthday on 8 May. The difference in the dates was explained to me in terms of life in the Jewish community at the time. Nearly all the Jewish babies were delivered by a midwife named Mrs Shillman. To get to the place where births were registered, one had to walk a good distance. This was not easy for Mrs Shillman, so she would wait until she could register a few births at the same time. So when she got to the registry office, all the babies were given that day's date as their birth date. I am certain that I was born on 8 May, but naturally took the official date as the one on my birth certificate.

Ada Shillman was a remarkable woman. She came from Lithuania to Cork around the late 1880s. She studied for a diploma in midwifery in Cork, and then moved with her husband to Dublin in 1892. For forty years she was one of the busiest midwives in the city and worked closely with Dr Bethel Solomons, the first Jewish Master of the Rotunda Hospital. After her death in 1933 Bethel Solomons wrote to her son Bernard, 'She was one of the best midwives I have ever met.'

There were fifty-eight houses in Greenville Terrace, and in the 1920s there were seventeen Jewish families living in that street. On our side, going down on the left from South Circular Road, lived the Ordmans, ourselves (the Harrises), the Eppels, the Weiners, the

Bauers, the Rubensteins (no relation to the Rubensteins of Clanbrassil Street), the Taylors, the Fines, Zunda Eppel and the Rathouses. On the opposite side, going up Greenville Terrace, lived the families Bera Levy, Gutkin, Brodie, Lovat and White. The Sevitt family who lived in Greenville Terrace later went to live in Carlisle Street off the South Circular Road. The Preager family also lived on our street, and they moved to Dufferin Avenue around the corner from Greenville Terrace.

My earliest clear memories are from 1920 when I was five years old. I remember watching British soldiers parading in the yard of the barracks opposite Greenville Terrace. I was with my friend John Kelly. Through the railings we were able to see the soldiers changing guard and marching around the parade grounds. When they were going through the side gates some of them gave us money, which we spent on sweets in the shop facing the barracks.

I remember the Black and Tans in 1921. They were called the Black and Tans because of the clothes they wore. I remember them walking up our street when there was a curfew, and the people had to remain indoors from early evening until dawn. Most people waited outside their houses until the Tans came near, and then went inside. But there was one lady who did not go inside when they approached. I remember her well. Her name was Nelly Kelly and her younger brother John was one of my best friends. Nelly was jeering the Tans and did not go inside until one of them threatened her with his rifle. When we went back into our house we heard loud bangs coming from the house next door. From the noise that was going on, it sounded as though they were playing football. In fact, they were kicking around a football that they found in one of the rooms. One of the boys of that family, the Clerys, was a footballer, and he played for Bohemians Football Club.

When I first saw the Black and Tans I was only six years of age. I knew that they were a rough crowd and that everyone seemed to be afraid of them, but I had no idea of why they were in Dublin and why they came down our street sometimes. Years later, I heard people using very strong language about them. They would describe them as 'a murderous lot of criminals that were sent over by the British government . . . jail birds and mercenaries sent over to deal with the Irish Republican Army and other factions opposed to British occupation . . . merciless thugs who caused untold damage throughout the country.'

I found out that there was a lot of truth in those words, and years later I found out some of the actual facts. The Black and Tans were former British soldiers, recruited by advertisement for service in Ireland as reinforcements for the RIC (Royal Irish Constabulary). They arrived at the height of the War of Independence and their job was to do everything possible to destroy the Irish Republican Army and supporters in the civilian population. They were paid ten shillings a day. When they arrived they were dressed in Khaki jackets with black trousers and cap, and the people promptly named them 'the Black and Tans'. By the time they left Ireland in 1922 they were detested by everybody, including many of the British soldiers. The Irish have long memories and they have not forgotten the raids, burnings and torture suffered by so many at the hands of the Black and Tans.

Greenville Terrace faced Wellington (now Griffith) Barracks. St Alban's Road, Raymond Street, Washington Street and Dufferin Avenue ran parallel to Greenville Terrace. These streets all faced the barracks and people could see the comings and goings of the soldiers and the Black and Tans. I remember one morning seeing some Republicans who had been rounded up. I counted ten of them. They were walking up our street with their hands up in the air, and there was an armoured car behind them with three soldiers on either side. They were being marched to the barracks, but I don't know what happened to them. I can also remember watching a man in a kneeling position at the end of Washington Street, shooting at the barracks. After firing a number of shots he got up and walked away, unperturbed that he was being watched by several of us boys. He just put the gun into his coat pocket and went away.

I always knew that more than one Jewish person was killed during the Troubles in Dublin, and when I was visiting my doctor Kenny Harris and told him that I was writing a book about my memories of growing up in Dublin, I mentioned that I thought that some Jewish people were killed by accident in Dublin during the Troubles in 1920 or 1922. I said that a person named Khan was one, but I was astounded when he said that his grandfather, Harris Abrahams, was also shot, and then told me the story as he knew it.

His grandfather had a clothing business on Lower Ormond Quay. At that time there was a curfew on. People had to be off the streets by a certain time and he was going home during the curfew. Whether he thought the curfew did not include people like himself or he did not know about it at all, he left his place of business and started to walk across Capel Street Bridge. He was called upon to halt but panicked and began to run. Shots were fired and he was killed.

When he did not return home, the family naturally worried, but it was not until three days later they found that he was in the city morgue with no identification papers on him. At the coroner's inquest, the verdict was death by accident.

It was some time in 1922 that the British army began to leave Ireland. People on both sides of the South Circular Road watched in complete silence as the troops marched out from the barracks. They were on their way to the docks where they boarded the ships to take them back to England. They were loaded down with heavy equipment and marched behind tanks and armoured cars. How could a little boy of seven understand the significance of what was happening? As I stood with the crowds, I did not know that what I was seeing was part of the history I would read about later on. And listening to the shelling of the Four Courts, I knew nothing about the Civil War that was just beginning and was to last until the following year.

After the Civil War in Ireland, unemployment was rife and I can recall seeing some of the older Jewish boys saying goodbye to people at the end of our street in Greenville Terrace, for six young men whom I knew were emigrating to America to seek their fortune. These were Arthur Sevitt, Hymie Gutkin, Samuel Taylor, who lived in Greenville Terrace, Louis Ginsberg and Arthur Sharp, who lived in Dufferin Avenue, and the sixth, Henry Jackson, who lived in Washington Street.

I was told that money was raised to pay their fares plus extra for them to live on until they got jobs.

I never thought any more about it until some years later when I heard that of the six who went away, three had returned. Arthur Sharp was given a job by a relation to manage a furniture shop in Mary Street. Some time later he married Bloomie Rubinstein and joined her in the catering business. Arthur Sevitt became an agent for a radio firm which sold radios called, I think, 'Philco'. I remember my parents bought one from him. He married a lady from England and eventually went to live there. The third, Henry Jackson, proved to be the most successful of the three. I did not hear anything about the three who stayed on and they never returned to Dublin.

I remember Henry Jackson coming to our factory looking for an order for stationery. He was very persistent and would not leave until he got an order, and I understand it was the same with other Jewish firms. He was so successful in building up his business that he opened a shop in Dame Street, and later moved to a larger shop in George's Street. It was through sheer hard work that his business expanded and it was no surprise that it was taken over by the Hely Group, one of the largest stationery firms in Dublin.

I remember talking to Henry one day when I visited the company regarding the purchase of a calculating machine I was interested in, and he confided to me that what he missed most in the present business that he had enjoyed in his own shop was meeting and talking to people. I must say that he deserved his success as he was a most likable person. He was married to Gertie Leon (who now lives in England) and had three children, two girls and a boy, Stephen, whom I see from time to time, who is, like his late father, most friendly.

In the early 1920s, we were accustomed to seeing the lamplighters coming to light the gas lights on the street lamps with a flame attached to a long pole. By 1928, nearly all the shops and houses had electricity installed. Naturally, we were thrilled by the difference this made to our lives. All you had to do was touch the switch and the light came on. Up to then, we had gaslight and candles.

My parents were very orthodox. On the Sabbath we were not allowed to switch the electric light on or off. We would put on the lights before the Sabbath came in on the Friday afternoon. Before we went to bed, a non-Jewish boy or girl would come in to attend to the fire and switch off the lights. This person would stoke up the fire or sometimes put slack on it. Then on the Saturday morning someone would come in to add coal to the fire. We called the people who carried out these tasks the *Shabbos goys*. The *Shabbos goy* would be paid about sixpence on the Sunday. When the Sabbath was out, my father or one of the boys would have to say the relevant prayer before we could turn on the lights. Even today this practice is adhered to in orthodox homes, though I am sure the lights are on a time switch nowadays.

I have often wondered how on earth eight children and two parents managed to live in the house in Greenville Terrace where I was born. It may have been extended in recent years but in our time it was a small house. There were two bedrooms, a good-sized kitchen and a large front room where we sat around a big table for meals on Friday night and on Saturday when we came back from *shul*. My parents slept in this front room, and I can remember that there were two small cots in one corner where my younger brother Louis and my baby sister Sadie slept.

There was a sink in the kitchen where we washed ourselves. My parents had a large bowl and jug that my father used to fill with water that he heated up before he went to work in the morning. The toilet was outside and there was a coal shed beside it. There was a small garden where we used to keep hens and some ducks, and I remember that we also had a goose. Each of the bedrooms in the house had a fireplace, and I have a very clear memory of the Diamond Coal Company. There was a Mr Cohen who lived at the top of Leinster Road and he used to call to our house to take the order for coal. I am not sure if he owned the company. I remember the price of coal was twenty-one shillings per ton. Mr Cohen was a small and very pleasant man.

There was a range in the kitchen in which the fire was always kept going. We also had a gas cooker. In the winter there was always a fire in my parents' room. It seemed to keep the house warm along with the range in the kitchen. In my parents' room I can recall a piano in a corner that my sister Leah played. It was certainly a small house for such a large family. We must have got on very well with each other because I can't remember any arguing or fighting. I know that the situation was eased somewhat when my sister Leah got married to Sam Farbenbloom about 1925 and my brother Sam married Hetty Sabin a year later.

I can remember my mother giving money to Hymie, Harry and myself to go to the Iveagh Baths, which were only about ten minutes from our house. We had to pay nine pence each to have a bath. When we paid our money we were given a towel and a small bar of soap that we always brought back home. We usually had to wait about fifteen minutes for our bath. There must have been at least fifteen to twenty cubicles. In each one of these there was an iron bath that was cleaned every time after it was used. You were allowed about fifteen minutes to have your bath, and I enjoyed splashing around in the lovely hot water. My parents used to go to the Iveagh Baths in the evening. When my two brothers and I went, we always had to bring back the tickets to prove to our mother that we did have a bath.

I also remember my mother taking me to the Dún Laoghaire Baths, where she would have a hot seaweed bath and I had an ordinary bath. I think my mother suffered from rheumatism, which was a very common complaint in those years. She went at least once a month for the hot seaweed bath. She was told that it was good for her, and I know she really enjoyed it. She would always take one of the children with her when she went to Dún Laoghaire.

I remember a large tin bath that was used for bathing my younger brother and sister. It was in the kitchen, and when one of my young sisters was having her bath none of the boys was allowed to go into the kitchen. The same applied to the girls when my younger brother was having a bath. I must confess that I never even thought about it at the time, but I realise now that my mother must have been very prudish.

Looking back to those years, we had great contentment at home. I cannot remember any real arguments or my father ever having to rebuke us, or for that matter my mother having to tell us off. I never felt that we were poor. We may not have had money, but neither did we have many desires at that age. We were always well fed and well clothed. In fact my mother never appeared annoyed if any of us came home and didn't like what she had cooked. She just gave us something else. We came home at different times, and I never ever heard my mother saying, 'You can eat what I have cooked or do without, because I am not going to cook individual meals.' The only times when the whole family sat down together was on Friday night and on Saturday when the men came back from the synagogue, and of course on all the festivals.

When we were growing up, conversation between the children

in our house was conducted in English. While my mother had a reasonable knowledge of English, she usually spoke to us in Yiddish, and on Friday nights and *Shabbos* when we all sat down together for meals she always spoke to my father in Yiddish. So we got to understand Yiddish without actually using it when we talked together. I can remember my mother addressing my father as 'So-ber'. This must have been some term of endearment in Russian, but none of us knew the meaning of it. There were also times when my mother spoke to my father in Russian, particularly if she didn't want us children to know what she was saying.

We had many religious people coming to our home, and the conversation was always in Yiddish. When a visitor spoke to me, I was often asked to reply in English. It would have been rude to reply in Yiddish, because they wanted to learn English, and it never struck me to do this. As far as I can remember, Yiddish continued to be spoken in our home until my mother died. I have always been grateful to her for giving me the ability to converse with any stranger who could only speak Yiddish. It is a very rich language and there are many expressions that do not have the same impact when translated into English.

Sometimes, in Greenville Terrace, when my mother decided to have a meat dinner on the Friday night, a hen was caught and my brother Harry or I would bring the hen to be killed at the local Jewish abattoir. The *shochet* (authorised slaughterer of animals, according to *kosher* dietary law requirements) would cut the hen's throat with a special knife, so sharp that the hen would not feel it. Then he would place the hen in a receptacle with a narrow end to let the blood run into special containers. When the hen was dead, you could have it plucked for four pence. But there were many times when I plucked the hen myself and was able to keep the money, which came in handy when I wanted to go to the pictures.

All fowl and all animals had to be killed in this way to be deemed *kosher*. The *shochet* was authorised and supervised by the Rabbi, and he had to be familiar with the many rules relating to *kosher* food. The knife had to be checked regularly to make sure that there were no defects on the cutting edge. It is said that this form of killing is painless. Occasionally, when she was preparing the hen to be cooked, my mother would notice a lump on some part of the hen's innards. When this happened I would have to bring the hen to Rabbi Herzog, who was the Rabbi at the time. He would examine the hen carefully in order to decide if the lump would cause the hen to be *trayf* (not conforming to Jewish standards). If it was *trayf*, my mother would give it to a non-Jewish person. There was nothing wrong with the hen itself; it was just that we could not eat it.

When I was growing up in Greenville Terrace, I was always the one who had to bring boots and shoes to Mr Atkins to be mended. I don't know why I was always chosen for this job, but I never liked going because he seemed to me to be a very fearsome looking man. He worked in the front room of his two-storey house in Clanbrassil Street, facing Lombard Street. When I went in he would be crouched over his shoemaker's last, hammering nails into the boots, taking each nail out of his mouth. Maybe that is what made me afraid of him, watching him do that. One day, taking up one of the boots I brought him, he asked me 'Are these your boots?' When I mumbled 'Yes', he said, 'You're wearing down the heels too quickly, and I'm going to put studs on them to make them last longer.' I was afraid even to say Yes or No.

Another reason why I was afraid of him was because I knew he drove the black hearse that carried coffins to Dolphin's Barn cemetery. He would be sitting on a seat at the front of the hearse, driving the horse. When he died this task was taken over by his son who was a beadle in the Adelaide Road Synagogue and always wore a top hat while driving the hearse. The use of a horse-drawn hearse was discontinued after World War II and a motor hearse was used thereafter.

Most of the boys I played with were given nicknames. Dave became 'Bimbo', Aaron was called 'Ucky', Louis got the name 'Lubs', Jack was 'Jabella', Lionel was 'Gluer', Simon was called 'Saps', Joe was called Jóulé, then there was Geoffrey who got called 'Podge'. And what about me? The headmaster in Catherine's called me 'Smiler Harris'; some other names I had to answer to were 'Nicholas Nickleby' (which came about because I used to get tips on horses and pass them on, and one was Nicholas Nickleby that won a race paying twenty to one), Nicky, Nat, and as my Hebrew name is Nachum, they concocted a rhyme in my honour: 'Nockim up, Nockim down, Nockim all around the town.' Now I am called Nick.

When we lived in Greenville Terrace we had a dog and a cat. The dog was called Nelly or Nell, and she answered to both names. She was of mixed breed, but mostly Alsatian. She was very docile. She would allow children to play with her and would never bite or growl at them. Nelly and the cat had grown up together and they were great friends. Often, when she was sleeping, the cat would curl up between her legs to keep warm. And when Nelly was eating, she didn't object if the cat sniffed at her food. But when the cat was eating, she would hiss loudly if Nelly came anywhere near her.

My friend Phil Ordman who lived next door once told me that when he was very young he used to play with Nelly. He could put his hand in her mouth and was never afraid to pull her ears. Then his family moved to Victoria Street, and some years later we also moved to Victoria Street to a house nearly opposite to the Ordmans. When he saw Nelly outside our door and went over to pat her, she growled as if to say 'Where were you all these years?' It was a sad day for all of us when she died. We never tried to replace her.

In those days of coal fires and coal ranges for cooking, my mother was kept quite busy preparing meals for the children. We had a maid who came every Thursday for nearly the whole day. She was paid one shilling and her food for the day. Her name was Mary and I think she only worked for Jewish people. There were other maids also who worked for Jewish families and after some time they knew what *kashrut* (strict observance of *kosher* laws) was all about. Some of these women were able to cook many kinds of Jewish meals.

My parents paid rent of a few shillings a week. Our landlord owned a number of houses on Greenville Terrace, and he and his eldest son carried out any repairs that were needed. I remember seeing articles of furniture outside a house at the end of Greenville Terrace and I thought that the people were moving. It turned out that they were evicted for not paying the rent. I cannot be sure that the house was one of those owned by our landlord, but I know that he was not popular.

Later on, when my parents decided to move from Greenville Terrace to Victoria Street, there were many people offering to pay my mother 'key money' to let them move into the house. There was no such thing as a lease. Tenants could pass on the house to anyone they wished, and as long as the new tenant paid the rent there was nothing the landlord could do about it.

I remember my mother (who had all the say) giving the house to a Mr and Mrs Solomons, the parents of Kopul Rosen who later founded Carmel College in London. She would not take any money from them, because they had very little at that time. Mr Solomons used to go to people's homes selling haberdashery articles. Henry, one of the sons, was very involved in B'nai B'rith—a Jewish organisation whose aim was to promote goodwill amongst people— before he emigrated to Australia with his wife (an English girl called Sybil Lyon). Before going to London, Kopul taught Hebrew to the girls in Zion Schools.

The Solomons parents had a tragic death. To keep food hot for the *Shabbos*, orthodox people used to leave a gas light burning with a cover of metal so that the naked flame would not be in contact with the pot the food was in. My mother always did this, right up to the time she died. The food for the *Shabbos* was prepared on Friday before *Shabbos* came in. It appears that in the Solomons' home the gas light was left on as usual to keep the *Shabbos* dinner warm; possibly a door was then opened and caused a draught which put out the gas light, and they were both found dead in bed from gas inhalation.

Something that will never leave me was the revolting smell from Keefe's the 'knackers'. This was a factory situated not far from where we lived and they manufactured glue. I have a very clear recollection of Keefe's men examining a dead horse that was lying in a field called The Tenters at the end of our road. I don't know how the horse happened to be there, but it had probably been dumped. I can still see the two men putting chains around the horse's head and body and winching it onto a flat cart. I never found out until a long time later that glue was made from horses' hides and bones. How the people living nearby endured the smell, I will never know. I can even get it as I write. It penetrated the houses in the whole area and was even worse in the summer time when there was no breeze to take it away. When we eventually moved to Victoria Street around 1928–9, we were no longer affected by the overpowering odour from the 'knackers'.

In Victoria Street we were delighted to have so much more space. We had three bedrooms, a kitchen, a dining room, a living room, an indoor toilet and a bathroom with hot and cold running water. We also had a large back garden and an outdoor toilet. Shortly after we went to live in Victoria Street my brother Hymie left to set up his own home when he married Ruby Isaacs. That left my sisters Jean and Sadie sharing the bedroom to the front of the house and Harry and Louis sharing the back bedroom, with me occupying the small room downstairs.

When we moved in I noticed that there was a small annexe

attached to the front room. I did not know what its purpose was but I immediately asked my mother could I have it for my bedroom. I was delighted when she agreed. A small bed, a chest of drawers and a chair were put in. I was thrilled, because it was mine. It also had a window, and I took great pride in having a room for myself even though it was small.

Shortly afterwards, when I started working, I saw a small wardrobe for sale in a shop called Cavendish's in Grafton Street. It was priced £5 12s 6d and I vowed to myself that I would buy it. I was always thrifty and even though I was earning only two shillings and six pence per week I put aside one shilling every week out of my wages. I was the one in the factory who had to go on all the messages. I would deliver suits to shops and I was also sent to the Dublin Woollen Mills beside the Ha'penny Bridge to buy threads, linings, etc. On my first visit to the Woollen Mills I noticed when I got the receipt that for every £1 you spent you received a shilling discount. I took advantage of that and whenever I was sent for a purchase I would save the receipt. I even picked up some dockets that I saw lying on the floor and was thrilled to receive the extra shillings.

When I had five shillings saved I went to the shop. I picked out the wardrobe I had set my eyes on and gave the sales assistant the five shillings as a deposit. I remember the assistant asking me if I wanted to pay off the balance on hire purchase. I could hardly answer him because my thoughts were on the wardrobe, knowing that I had bought something of my own for the first time. Anyway, I said 'No, I would prefer to pay the balance as soon as possible.' I continued to collect the dockets at the Woollen Mills, and I even went into the shop whenever I passed by to see if I could find discarded dockets. As well as this, I earned money by buying suit lengths for friends and adding an extra few shillings to the amount; I also kept the discount. My friends did not complain, because they got the suit lengths at wholesale price.

When I told my mother that I was buying the wardrobe she offered to buy it for me, but I said that I wanted to buy it myself. When I told her I had already saved three pounds she was very impressed and gave me the additional amount that I needed. Needless to say I was over the moon, and I rushed off to Cavendish's to pay the balance and to tell the salesman when to deliver the article. It was a proud day for me when I came home from work to see the wardrobe in the hall looking so elegant. One of my brothers helped me to carry it into my room. It fitted as perfectly as if it had been made to measure. It had shelves on one side and a space to hang clothes on the other side. Every morning when I woke up I looked at it with delight.

A friend once asked me what my parents did for entertainment. I remember that they had many friends who came around to chat with them about various topics. But I never heard any conversations about where they came from. Thinking back on those conversations, it seems strange that nobody mentioned anything about their earlier lives. My parents' friends had also come from other countries. It seems that there was a taboo on talking about life before they came to Ireland. My parents never spoke about their own parents, or even mentioned if they had brothers or sisters at home. At the time we were busy with our own activities and never thought to ask about their life in Russia. Usually the history of families is passed down to their children, but not in our case, and very few of our friends knew of their own parents' upbringing.

When we did not have visitors, we listened to music. Nearly every Jewish household had a gramophone and records. There was a wide selection of Jewish cantors, such as Moshe Stern, Moshe Koussevitsky and others. The songs they sang were full of emotion and my parents listened to their singing with pure joy. We also had many opera stars singing some of the great arias. We listened to Gigli, Caruso, Richard Tauber and others. We had some John

McCormack records that were great favourites of my mother. Bing Crosby and Dean Martin came later. We often listened also to my eldest sister, Leah, who was a talented pianist. She played many classical pieces, and I can remember seeing people standing outside our house in Greenville Terrace listening to her playing.

Over the years, the most frequently played record was 'My Yiddish Momma' by Sophie Tucker. That song brought tears to my mother's eyes. Even my father blew his nose as if to disguise his feelings. That one record must have reminded them of the thousands of Jewish people who left Russia and their families. But why did they not talk to us about their *heim* (home)? I also have that record. I think of my own mother, and I am not ashamed to admit that the tears well up when I play it. The Mommas and *Bubbas* (grandmothers) of those years left an indelible mark on their *kinder* (children). Their whole life was for their children.

My mother was a great draughts player, and usually enjoyed a game after our *Shabbos* meal. She was the champion player in the home. Nobody could beat her. She also liked playing a card game called 'Pisha Paysha' that must have originated in Eastern Europe. I played many a game with her. There was no skill in it but it was a good way to relax for half an hour. I am sure that only Jewish people know this game.

My earliest memory of seeing a doctor was when Dr Wigoder came to our house when my sister Jean had the measles. He also came to attend one of us for some illness that I cannot remember. He was a small man with a big heart. He was in every way a family doctor who would come out at any time, day or night, to take care of members of the community. He was also a very learned man, and the name of Dr Wigoder was to be remembered and respected. He will always be remembered for his favourite remark, 'I will give you a pill and you will be alright.'

Dr Wigoder was succeeded by Jack Robinson. He also would

attend a patient at any time, day or night. When he was at some function with his wife, he would leave immediately if he was called. He would always greet you with an encouraging smile and a handshake, and it was the same if you had to visit him at his surgery. He was a devoted family doctor, who loved his patients and his work. He was also an accomplished violinist, and gave violin lessons before he qualified as a doctor. From the violin lessons, he earned money to enable him to study medicine. One day when he was living at Victoria Street a young boy knocked at the door, which was opened by Jack's mother. He was asked to come in, and Mrs Robinson called out to Jack, who was upstairs, 'Professor, you have a pupil.'

There was a chemist named Misstear on the corner of Clanbrassil Street. He was not Jewish but had a very large Jewish custom, being right in the Jewish area. He dispensed all the medicines and people trusted him because of the interest, help and advice he gave them. Many times I had to go to him with a prescription, and I can remember how he would tell me what to tell my mother about how to use the medicine. Maybe he knew that not many of the Jewish women were able to read. How right he was at that time. I have always remembered him as a very kind man who had time like a doctor to listen to you.

There were many Jewish-owned chemist shops in other parts of the city. I must give pride of place to Mushatt's of Francis Street in the Liberties, the oldest part of Dublin. Louis Mushatt was a dispensing chemist in the early 1920s, when chemists had to compound doctors' prescriptions. Louis was helped in the shop by his brother Harold, who was not a qualified chemist. They made up their own lotions and ointments to cure all ailments. People came to Mushatt's from far and wide. Louis was looked on as a 'doctor' and had a sympathetic ear for everyone who came to him. Whole families would come, and were able to tell Louis or Harold that their mothers and grandmothers were treated by Mushatts. If Harold was out, their sister Doris would help Louis in the shop.

Harold Mushatt deserves special mention for the part he played in the Jewish community. His lifetime of service to the Adelaide Road *shul* was recognised when he was made 'Life Councillor'. He had a great knowledge of the Jewish rituals and was always available to give any help that was needed in the synagogue. He was also a founder member of the Jewish Museum. He died in December 1994 aged well over eighty.

# 3 The Heart of the Community

Clanbrassil Street was the heart of the Jewish community. It catered for all the Jewish people in Dublin, and for at least 95 per cent of them it was within walking distance. From early morning to late at night there was movement in the street, with shopkeepers bringing in supplies in the morning and then tidying up in the evening. Hours didn't mean anything—they were used to working long hours. In the 1920s, and indeed until after World War II, very few people had fridges, so they had to shop nearly every day for food. I remember we had a 'food press' in the garden. It was made with wire mesh to let the air in and keep the food as fresh as possible.

Clanbrassil Street was alive with shoppers coming to the street or going home laden with parcels. I remember the feverish activity there in the 1920s and 1930s, on days leading up to the Jewish New Year or on other festivals. To see the women with their baskets full of food would make you think they were laying in supplies for a siege. The preparations and the shopping went on for days. In that period, strangers who happened to walk through the fairly narrow street might wonder where they were when they saw bearded men clutching parcels or passed groups of women talking loudly in a strange language. They might hear 'Happy New Year' or *Leshana tova* (the same greeting in Yiddish) being called to people on the other side of the road. They might ask why people were saying 'Happy New Year' in September.

For at least two weeks before *Pesach* (Passover), stocks of Passover food had to bought and stored away so that it did not come into contact with food eaten during the rest of the year. Lists were made out and trips were made to Clanbrassil Street each day and even twice a day. Shopkeepers had to separate the food brought in for Passover from the food they were still selling. The food for the Passover was mostly imported from England. It must have been a nightmare for them, and no doubt their families had to help out. Jewish readers will understand why the food for the eight days of Passover is prepared in a different way to the food eaten for the rest of the year. The actual food is basically the same, but the method of cooking it is different and some of the ingredients used are different.

The machinery in the food factories has to be thoroughly cleaned to comply with the *kashrut* regulations. In fact some of the larger food manufacturers have machines that are only used for the Passover. Food manufactured for Passover must be stamped to say that it is strictly *kosher* for *Pesach*, and vegetables and fish are the only food that Jewish people can buy from non-Jewish shops. Barley, wheat, oats, rye and all cereals used for baking with leaven are forbidden and must be removed from the house before the first night of Passover. All these are *chomatz* (not *kosher* for Passover). Milking has to be supervised. The container for the milk has to be scoured properly and must not come in contact with other articles.

The fact that Clanbrassil Street was the only place the community could purchase Passover food could lead to chaotic scenes as people rushed into the shops to be served. Easter and Passover usually fall around the same time, so the children had holidays from school and were able to go with their mothers to carry home the boxes of food, including the *matzo* (unleavened bread) that we eat for the whole of *Pesach*. As very few people had any kind of transport, everything had to be carried. My brother Harry and I went with our mother to help her. Even our younger sister Jean came along also.

It was unbelievable what went on with people shouting to be served. Non-Jews passing through the area must have thought the people were fighting each other when they saw the carry-on. Many of the shopkeepers were exhausted and must have wondered was it worth it. Every Jewish shop had the same experience. The women always had to do the shopping themselves because their husbands were out at work, except on Sundays. When they finished buying the groceries they went to the butchers for their supplies of meat, and the same conditions prevailed there. We kept hens in our back garden both in Greenville Terrace and in Victoria Street, so my brother Harry and I used to bring two hens to the abattoir to be killed and then eaten during the eight days of *Pesach*. Being young boys we did just what we were told to do, and the scenes we witnessed in Clanbrassil Street during the days before *Pesach* did not register with us. We assumed that they were part of the normal way of life with Jewish people.

When Passover ended and more tranquil days returned to Clanbrassil Street, people visiting the street had more time to gossip about current affairs. Shopkeepers were able to bring back the stocks of food that had been taken off the shelves. Foodstuffs that were bought specially for *Pesach* were left on the shelves as they could be eaten during the rest of the year. I remember seeing two men having an animated conversation outside Ordman's shop. I have no doubt that they were discussing how *meshugge* (mad, crazy) some of the people were, pushing and shoving to be served before the Passover. But then come Thursday and Friday, when the *Shabbos* came in around 4 pm in the winter months, the women came back to the street for their supplies. Shopping in Clanbrassil Street never stopped.

Clanbrassil Street was where Jewish people heard what was going on in the community. They would hear about births. They would hear who had passed away and what time the funeral was to take place, and then they would inform their neighbours. They would also hear who was ill. It was like the bush telegraph. It started off with members of the community who attended an early morning service in the synagogue, where they learned of the death of a Jewish person from a member of the Burial Society who would go there to announce the death. The member of the Burial Society would also bring word to the Jewish shops in Clanbrassil Street. In a very short time the news spread through the community. It also gave time to the women friends of the family of the deceased to prepare the ancient ritual of the Jews, and to have hard-boiled eggs and bagels ready to be eaten when the mourners returned from the funeral. This ritual is observed in most Jewish homes to the present day.

Nearly all Jews mourned the death of a member of the family for one week (*Shivah*). At various times during the day they would sit on stools, especially when prayers were being said. Food was brought to the home of the mourners during the week of mourning, as they were not supposed to cook any meals. Friends and acquaintances would come during the day to keep them company and wish them 'long life'. This is an age-old custom that is now being relaxed, with prayers being said only in the evening. It is a custom which helps the bereaved to cope with the initial stage of grieving.

Very few private homes had telephones, so when people were shopping in Clanbrassil Street they were able to get up-to-date news about anything that was happening in the community. Being the first to bring the news to the shops also gave people a sense of superiority. Some non-Jews, seeing the Jewish women carrying baskets of food from the grocers or the butchers, might have got the impression that the Jews in the 1930s were an affluent society. But they were wrong. Most of the customers had accounts in the shops and paid off their debts from week to week.

Many of those same women were receiving weekly support from the Board of Guardians, a charitable organisation that members of the community paid into through the synagogues. Very many families only managed to get by with the help of the Board, which was always completely confidential. Some people might be surprised to know that even in this affluent age there are still members of the community who are helped in this way.

Besides the help given by the Board of Guardians, women from various charitable societies would visit some homes on Thursdays and Fridays to make sure that they had food for the Sabbath. My mother-in-law was one of those women who helped out by giving money to poorer women in Clanbrassil Street every week. Many families were brought up in rooms in Clanbrassil Street and elsewhere, and there was no shame in being helped. Food and heat were the priorities for these people. It is part of the Jewish culture to help your fellow human beings. There were also many non-Jews who received help from the various societies.

Some years ago the Board of Guardians were the recipients of a legacy from a non-Jewish person, and it is not generally known why it was given. It will go to show how an act of kindness by one person of our community to another who happened not to be Jewish was rewarded many years later.

I am sure that there are many older members of the community who remember Dawson's Amusement Arcade in Bray during the war years, and the pleasure many of us got from the different games such as hoopla and the shooting gallery. I am sure many of us remember sitting down to the game of 'housey housey', now called 'Bingo'.

There was a Mr John Currid who may have worked for Mr Dawson, but he wanted to set up his own amusement arcade. He went to Domigan's on Merchant's Quay, a firm dealing in small goods of the kind he wanted, but was refused credit there, as he was by Smyths, a few yards away.

In between these two wholesalers was a small warehouse owned by Wolfe Freedman. John Currid took a chance and went in there to see if they would help him to set up his venture. There he met Barney Lewis, brother of Rabbi Lewis. Barney was the manager of the firm and when John Currid explained what he wanted, Barney agreed to back him and John Currid opened an amusement arcade in Talbot Street off O'Connell Street. He continued the business and some years later went to England, and as far as was known, no further contact was made.

Then, in 1985, the Board of Guardians received a letter from a solicitor acting on behalf of John Currid to say that he had died. He had not married and seemed not to have any family. He left close on three million pounds, and to the Board of Guardians he gave nearly three quarters of a million pounds for the help he received from the Jewish people of Dublin. Each year on the anniversary of his death, prayers are read out in the synagogue in his memory.

The period from the 1920s to the 1940s was a difficult time for most members of the community, and being poor was not a shame. Everybody worked hard to make a living and give their children a good education. Jewish women loved to have a son become a doctor. I can remember walking past Zion Schools one day when classes ended, and seeing children buying sweets from a Jewish woman. She had the sweets on a tray, and she had a small attaché case on the ground in which she had additional supplies. This was just one example of the sacrifices that Jewish people made to give their sons a better chance in life than they had themselves. I can tell you that the son of the woman selling sweets did in fact become a doctor.

Many Jewish men were helped greatly by a friendly and sympathetic bank manager in the Northern Bank on the South Circular Road. His name was Mr McCormack, and he allowed many of them to go over their limit. He had good judgement and I don't think anyone ever let him down. But I do know that when the banks closed their doors on Friday afternoon at 3 pm there were a lot of relieved men who at least had Saturday and Sunday to rest and did not need to worry until Monday, when they used all efforts to meet the commitments of the next week.

In those days women had no say with regard to any decisions

concerning the community. It was the men's prerogative to lay down the rules and regulations, and the women had no choice but to comply. It was a hard life for everybody, and especially for women. I can remember my own mother washing clothes with the help of a scrubbing board, and pressing them when dry with a small black iron that she would heat over a gas light. Between looking after the house and in some cases large families, the work of many women was sheer drudgery. I'm sure their thoughts must have gone back to their young days when they watched their own mothers doing the same work, but in worse conditions under a hostile regime. At least in Ireland they were free from anti-Semitic attacks. To my mind, the women played a most important role in the community without ever receiving due recognition.

It was also a hard time for men who came to Ireland with no trades. Some went around collecting scrap metal to sell to the scrap merchants. Others collected wool clippings from clothing factories. Clippings are small pieces of cloth that are left over when the materials are cut for the manufacture of clothes. The clippings were sold to rag merchants, many of whom were Jewish. When the war broke out, these wool clippings became quite valuable in the making of blankets. Cotton clippings were also collected and were used in the making of cleaning cloths. A good livelihood could be made collecting clippings, and a number of men had a horse and cart to collect them from the many clothing factories in the 1930s, and through the 1940s until after the war had ended.

A loan society headed by a Louis Levinson was set up to help some of the immigrants to start a business. Some men, who had managed to get a loan, began going to the poorer non-Jewish areas offering clothing or other articles for sixpence or one shilling per week. They were called 'the weekly men'. Fifty to a hundred pounds was sufficient to give them a start, and in most cases the loan was repaid. Eventually, years later, the 'weekly men' became moneylenders.

Women also became involved in money lending. This happened when a moneylender died and his wife carried on the business that he had started. It must be emphasised that these moneylenders played a part in helping people to have things they needed and would not be able to have otherwise. There are many non-Jews who will testify to this day that without the help their parents got from the money-lenders, they would not have been able to cope. I have heard glowing reports of kindness from families who got into difficulties and were helped by the 'Jewman'. There is no doubt that from that period came the credit business of today. There was never any record of a moneylender taking someone to Court for non-payment of a debt. The debt was just written off.

People from every sector of the community shopped in Clanbrassil Street, and everything they needed could be supplied by the shopkeepers there. The bakery shop owned by the Weinrocks was in Clanbrassil Street. The actual bakery was in Rosedale Terrace, right behind the shop. *Challa* (a braided loaf used on *Shabbos*), bagels and cakes were sold in the shop. I remember a Mr Moisel, who worked for the Weinrocks, driving a horse and cart down our street, and the aroma of fresh bread wafting in the air. The cart was full of dark brown loaves baked in a full moon shape. A large tarpaulin covered the bread. Mr Moisel would come once a week, usually on Sunday morning, and then move on to the other nearby streets.

There was another bakery in St Kevin's Parade, owned by a Mr Goldberg. He baked and sold bread and he provided another service also. People brought prepared bread to him and he baked it for them. In the side wall of his house he had built an oven with an iron door and sufficient space to bake a quantity of bread. He would push the bread into the oven with a flat iron pole. I remember bringing the Sabbath bread, *challa*, and cinnamon rolls to him, and then calling back to collect them when they were baked. As far as I can recall, Weinrock's and Goldberg's were the only two *kosher* bakeries in Dublin. My mother usually baked her own bread. I remember her waiting for the yeast dough to rise. It would be in a basin on the oven, but there must have been occasions when the oven was being used for other meals. When the dough was ready it was my job to bring it to Mr Goldberg to be baked.

When Weinrock's closed at the end of the 1920s, Clein's Bakery in Lennox Street was the only *kosher* bakery left to supply the entire community. While Weinrock's only baked bread, Clein's had a variety of different breads and cakes. Solomon and Malka Clein had come from Cork many years earlier to start the bakery in Dublin, and as their baking was of an excellent standard, it was popular with both the community and non-Jews alike. For over twenty years they served the community. After they died, the bakery was continued by other members of the Clein family, then sold to Sidney Benson, who had come over from Liverpool with his brother George after the war.

The Benson family had a large bakery in Liverpool and when the father retired from the business, the boys decided to come and live in Dublin. Both married Dublin Jewish girls; Sidney married Rae Taylor and George married Hennie Lipschitz.

It was expected that both Sidney and George would run the bakery, but George decided that he had had enough of the arduous work the bakery demanded and left Sidney to run the business alone. Sidney ran it for many years, until illness forced him to retire. In 1960 he sold it to Christy Hackett—who had been working in the business for many years—with the approval of the *Kashrut* Board (Jewish dietary committee), with the proviso that Christy would only use the ingredients laid down by the Board, to which he agreed. Thus, the last of the Jewish-owned bakeries, having run for nearly one hundred years, passed into non-Jewish hands.

Incidentally, George, who started up a business of his own with no connection to the bakery trade, took a great interest in community affairs, as well as joining the Board of Guardians, one of Dublin's oldest charitable societies. After years of service, he was elected President and served in that post from 1979 to 1986. He died in 1988, and his wife and three sons left Dublin to live in London. His brother Sidney and his wife went to live in London and Sidney died shortly afterwards.

There was a great relationship between Christy Hackett and the Jewish community. He was always very obliging and would cater for individual people. I know, because whenever my wife and I arranged to visit our daughter and family in London, I would ask Christy if he would bake two cinnamon logs with extra fruit to take there as our daughter was very partial to those logs. I must say that Christy never refused; in fact he said he would put a few cherries on top of the logs 'so that the staff in the shop would know who the cinnamon logs were for.'

Christy changed the name of the shop to 'Bretzel', which means 'bread stick', as eaten by the inhabitants of the Romanian province of Transylvania. In 1970, Christy's son Morgan joined his father in the bakery and soon more and more varieties of bread and cakes were added to the stocks. They also began supplying non-Jewish catering outlets as well as non-Jewish people, and on many a Sunday you would see people queueing outside the shop waiting to be served. The Bretzel Bakery was fast becoming very well known.

Sadly, Christy Hackett died in 1989 and Morgan continued supplying the community as before, but on one occasion when I was in the shop, he told me that he was not getting the support of the diminishing Jewish community. About this time, Rabbi Broder found defects amongst the ingredients used by Morgan in the baking procedure, and told him he could help him to find the correct ingredients that would conform to the *Kashrut* Board rules. However, Morgan decided that he did not wish to change his baking methods, despite being full of praise for Rabbi Broder and his offer to help. Thus, Rabbi Broder took it upon himself to make contact with a bakery that would supply bread which would be acceptable to the Board.

This ended a chapter in the Dublin Jewish Community for the supply of *kosher* bread from a bakery that had been regarded as an institution.

Morgan Hackett sold the bakery in 2001 due to health reasons, and it is still flourishing as the Bretzel under new ownership. The business was bought by a Dublin man named William Dastard. When I went to see him, I found that he had no experience in baking before acquiring the Bretzel. He was very excited by the challenge and determined to make a success of the undertaking. After only two weeks working alongside the original staff, he already had a good knowledge of the business. He was happy also to have been well received by many of the regular customers.

I told him about the history of the Bretzel and the role it had played in the Jewish community. I asked him if he would be interested in continuing to bake for the community if the conditions laid down by the Jewish authorities could be met. His response was very positive. He said he would check the baking capacity of the Bretzel and then perhaps consider the staff and time implications. Now I have to find out if the Rabbinate would be interested in renewing the relationship that the Jewish community had with the Bretzel for over eighty years.

My mother made *cholent* for *Shabbos*, and it was baked in Mr Goldberg's oven also. *Cholent* was a traditional meal that was eaten on the Sabbath. It must have brought back memories of the *heim* (their home place) where they saw their own mothers preparing the same kind of food. It is a mixture of meat, butter beans, potatoes, onions, sugar and dumplings. It was a substantial meal and would keep for a few days. As it took a long time to cook, I remember bringing a large pot of the *cholent* to Mr Goldberg on a Thursday, after Hebrew class. He would place the pot in the oven to cook overnight, to be collected when cool on Friday. When I brought the *cholent* back home, my mother would put the pot on a small gas light that was covered by a metal plate so that the flame would not be in contact with the pot itself. Religious people never cooked food on an open flame on the Sabbath. I must add that most Jewish people loved their food!

There were numerous butcher shops in Clanbrassil Street. On one side of the street we had Myer Rubenstein, Erlich's, Davis and Citron. On the opposite side we had Philly Rubenstein, Goldwater and Leopold (who only dealt with hens). A few doors away Isaac Goldwater sold fresh meat. Later, when Weinrock's gave up the bakery, Abe Samuels took over the shop premises for another butcher shop. We also had Baron's butcher shop in St Vincent's Street, just off Clanbrassil Street. As well as the butcher shop, Baron's had a delicatessen and sold meats, sausages, *wurst*, etc. We must have eaten a lot of meat in those days.

Then there were the grocery shops. We had Ordman's, Freedman's, Aranovitch, Buchalter's and Fine's. All of them were in Clanbrassil Street, and it was no wonder that it was often referred to as Little Jerusalem by the non-Jews also who bought food there. Venturing into grocery shops like Freedman's or Ordman's, you would immediately get the lovely smell of *schmaltz* and pickled herrings that were in barrels of brine. You would see the sticks of *wurst* hanging from a rail across the shop. Pickled cucumbers were in a container on the counter so that the customers could make their own choice. This was a never-ending scene and it provided a very colourful atmosphere.

Some people had grocery shops in their homes. These included Mrs Rick in Lombard Street, Jackson's in Washington Street, and Mrs Cohen in Walworth Road. I nearly forgot that there was another grocery shop called Jackson's in the middle of Clanbrassil Street. Mrs Jackson was the daughter of the Jacksons in Washington Street.

We also had a grocery shop at the end of Greenville Terrace, owned by Mrs Rathouse. And there was a well-stocked general food shop at the corner of Clanbrassil Street owned by a Mr Newman. This was the way people lived and the way they made a living.

Smullens and Alchmans supplied milk, and they had *kosher* milk that was specially supervised for *Pesach*. There were also milkmen who came to the houses every morning with fresh milk. My mother often bought a gallon or more milk to make *keiz* (cheese). It was left to stand in a large basin over the oven, and when it was ready my mother would skim off the cream. She would then put the *smethena* into a large cotton bag shaped to a point, to let the whey drip off, and we would have lovely cheese that we all enjoyed. Some of us would drink the whey that was left. I enjoyed the whey. When I got married I made the cheese as my mother made it, but this stopped when pasteurised milk was introduced.

There was a fish shop in Grantham Street off Camden Street. This shop was owned by Louis Danker who had lived in Belfast and married Annie Rubenstein, daughter of the legendary Myer Rubenstein. Louis smoked his own salmon and he had many non-Jewish customers. Many of us can remember the fish women who sold fish at the corner of Lombard Street. They used to be there, mainly on Thursdays, so that the Jewish women were able to buy the fish and prepare fish dinners for the Friday night. Very often they would go around the streets off the South Circular Road. We had moved to 38 Victoria Street and our neighbours were the Medalies. I have a vivid memory of one of the fish women offering fish that had not sold in Clanbrassil Street. She asked my mother for three shillings, which seemed to me to be good value for a lot of fish. Obviously, the fish women were accustomed to bargaining with their Jewish customers. I think my mother and Mrs Medalie each paid two shillings eventually for the fish they bought.

At the corner of Clanbrassil Street and Lombard Street there was a drapery shop owned by a Mrs Woolf. She was a stout woman, and it was clear that she was the one who ran the business because her husband always seemed to be lounging at the front of the shop. In later years Becky Fine opened a drapery shop that was well-stocked with ladies' and children's clothes.

Abe Robinson had a betting shop in St Vincent's Street. He lived in Carlow where the family had a furniture shop and a jewellery shop. As far as I know, the Robinsons were the only Jewish people living in Carlow. They were highly respected by the non-Jews of Carlow and many other towns. Joe and Maurice Mirrelson also had betting shops in Dublin. They had one at South Richmond Street, just at Kelly's Corner. I remember it well. I was given a tip by one of my father's customers and I went to Mirrelson's to place the bet. I was very embarrassed when my bet of two shillings each way was taken by one of the Mirrelson girls whom I knew—so much so that I was hoping my horse wouldn't win and then I would not have to go back to the shop. I cannot remember if my horse won or lost. I was never a gambler and that incident put me off betting on horses for a very long time. Years later the only bet I would place would be on the Grand National or the Derby.

We had Baigel's wine shop, and a number of people made mead and *kosher* wine. My father made mead for *Pesach*. Mrs Lewis in Clanbrassil Street and Mrs Jacobson in Oakfield Place also sold wine. Harris Baigel came from Lithuania early in 1900 with the help of two of his brothers who had come to Dublin a few years earlier. He married Eva Miller, a cousin of Becky Miller who lived in Longwood Avenue, South Circular Road. Their son Solly and I went to the same school, St Catherine's, and we were quite good friends. Solly also had a brother Gerald.

Solly told me that when his father arrived in Dublin, and wanted to learn English, he was advised to buy Chambers Dictionary. He proceeded to read through it page by page and when he came to the end he was able to hold a conversation in English. This system enabled him to learn English in a very short time! Harris Baigel sold wines and spirits along with a range of grocery items in his shop in Clanbrassil Street. Incidentally, he was the only Jewish person I knew who had a licence to sell spirits.

Solly's wife, Ettie Mann, was a very accomplished violinist. She was a pupil of Jack Robinson. She won gold and silver medals in the Feis Ceoil, and a gold medal and scholarship in the Royal Irish Academy of Music. She played in the Radio Eireann Symphony Orchestra, and she was frequently asked to play at Jewish and non-Jewish weddings. In 1953 Ettie gave birth in the Rotunda Hospital to two boys and a girl, the first Jewish triplets to be born in Ireland. The excitement was intense and the community responded with gifts of every description. Before the birth of the triplets, Solly and Ettie had a daughter called Moira. Moira decided that she wanted to be a doctor and qualified in 1975. She works with the Eastern Health Board looking after young children. She also finds time to be an officer of the St John's Ambulance Brigade, and attends sporting events to provide medical cover in case of accidents.

Moira married Jackie Woolfson, son of the very popular Abby and Hennie Woolfson. Abby came originally from Waterford where there was a small Jewish community that no longer exists. He married Hennie Rick who, in what might seem to be a coincidence, had twin brothers living in Dublin. Hennie's sister, Eileen, married Sid Cole who gave a lifetime of service to the Dublin community. Moira and Jackie had six children, but sadly Jackie died at the age of forty-five. His death left Moira to bring up the children on her own, which she has done extremely well.

For young people in the 1930s, Clanbrassil Street was our centre. We were forever going to the various shops asking for permission to stick up notices for dances or meetings. It was the only way we had of communicating information to the community at that time. I remember even asking Mr O'Reilly, who had a barber's shop next to Rubenstein's butcher shop, to let me put up a notice for one of our dances. Most of the Jewish boys went to Mr O'Reilly to get a haircut. We all thought he was very kind. He charged us one shilling for a haircut but always gave us back three pence for ourselves to spend.

People reading my account of life in Clanbrassil Street might be under the impression that it covered a large area. The street where all the Jewish-owned shops were situated is approximately 300 yards long, and these shops together with two or three others in nearby streets were responsible for supplying the needs of the entire Jewish community. The area was pretty run down, with buildings dating back to the Victorian era.

On the left side of the street, going down from South Circular Road, there were nine shops. Eight of them were in the food business; the exception was a watchmaker. Many Jewish families lived over the shops along that side of the street. On the right hand side, going down from South Circular Road, there were thirteen shops. Eleven of them were one after another as far as Lombard Street, and the remaining two were just past Lombard Street. Except for two drapery shops, all of these were also in the food business. As far as I can remember, there were no Jewish people living over the shops on this side of the street. In Vincent Street, just off Clanbrassil Street, there were two more shops and also the slaughter-house where hens were killed.

# 4 School Around the Corner

In 1921 I went to school. St Catherine's in Donore Avenue was a Protestant school about ten minutes from my home. I was in a mixed class for a while and was taught by a lady called Miss Spencer. I remember her very clearly, because it was she who sent me to the headmistress one day when I had been misbehaving. Instead of going to Miss Baily's room, I went into the toilet that was in the yard and stayed there for a few minutes. Then I went back to my own classroom and sat down at my desk. The teacher did not pass any remark and I thought I had got away with it. However, when the class resumed after lunch she said to me, 'By the way, Nathan Harris, did you go to Miss Baily when I sent you?' 'No,' said I. 'Then you had better go now,' she said. Off I went with my head down, realising that I was not as smart as I thought. But for the life of me, I cannot remember being punished. I would like to think that Miss Baily was amused.

Soon it was time to move to the boys' section of the school. Looking back on them now, I think these were some of the happiest years of my life. We had two masters, Mr Butler and Mr Abbot, and the headmaster was Dickie Griffin. They were dedicated teachers, and what I learned from them has always remained with me. They took great care in giving us a good grounding in all subjects. I remember Mr Butler getting us out of our seats, arranging us back to back and then firing all kinds of questions at us about arithmetic, geography, history, and other subjects. Mr Butler was very strict but very fair, and it was the same with the other teachers. There were competitions in class. The winner got a prize and occupied the front desk for a month. I am glad to say that I was first on two occasions.

We had singing lessons once a week. There were about thirty of us in the class and my seat was in the second last row. One day when we were singing, Mr Butler heard that somebody was way out of tune. To find the culprit, he made each of us sing a line of the song. When it was my turn and I sang the line, he said, 'What are you doing at the back of the class? You sit in the front.' I was already in the synagogue choir and was said to have a good voice, so from then on I sat in the front.

Some time later this promotion worked against me. While the master was putting questions to the boys at the back of the class, one of the boys in the front row passed a comic to me. I had it on my knees reading it when I heard the voice of the headmaster, Dickie Griffin, asking me if I was enjoying the comic. He had obviously looked over the partition that divided our class from his and saw what I was doing. Mr Butler was not amused and I got a few strokes of the leather strap on my hands. Now you know why I liked to sit at the back of the class!

I remember a day when I didn't want to go to school. I left home with my school bag and walked along by the canal. But I soon got bored because it was not much fun having nothing to do. So when schooltime was over I went home but said nothing to my mother about my escapade. As far as she was concerned I had gone to school and returned from school. But then I realised that I would need an excuse to give to the schoolmaster. I had a brainwave. Bernie Freeman, a boy in my class, had very good handwriting, so I asked him to write the excuse. It was accepted by the master without comment, but I never mitched again.

When we had a morning break in St Catherine's we didn't go home. If we had money, there was a bakery called Johnston Mooney and O'Brien's where we could buy jam tarts for two pence and lovely rock buns for the same price. The few pence we got for pocket money went a long way. I remember buying a penny's worth of Jacob's broken biscuits. We would get a large bag of a mixture of biscuits that were rejected because they were not perfect, and there could be lots of fig rolls and chocolate biscuits included. They were supposed to cost four pence per pound, but the shopkeeper would always give us a penny's worth more. Sixteen bulls' eyes cost a penny and large eating apples could also be bought for a penny.

The school arranged that classes of boys could go to factories. In Jacob's factory we were able to watch the biscuits actually being made. But we were always keen for the visit to end, because we knew that each of us would be given a small sample box of biscuits on the way out. The same thing happened in the factories where cigarettes, cigars and pipe tobacco were produced. Before leaving the Wills factory in Rialto and the Players factory in Phibsboro each of us received a sample box of cigarettes. We were only about eleven or twelve years old when we were given these samples. At that time there was no age limit for the sale of cigarettes, and people were not aware that smoking was dangerous to health. It was probably taken for granted that we would bring the samples home to our fathers or big brothers.

During the year, each class would be brought to the Spring Show in the Royal Dublin Society grounds at the beginning of May. There were displays of agricultural equipment produced by Irish and English manufacturers. There were stands where we used to get samples of biscuits, chocolate and sweets. We also roamed around the area where the cattle were judged, and one of the highlights was watching the horse-jumping. This took place in a large arena and teams from many countries took part. Back at school next day, we had to write an essay on what we saw on our visit to the Spring Show. I remember the teacher reading out part of an essay written by one of the boys. It was about a bull that gave so many gallons of milk per week. He did not name the boy, but of course we knew who he was.

During the summer the whole school went on an outing to the

seaside, at a place called Laytown. There was a wonderful strand there. Races were held, prizes were awarded and we were treated to buns, sandwiches and minerals. I don't remember winning any prizes, but I always looked forward to these outings, and the sun was always shining. Even though it was a Protestant school, there was a large number of Jewish children in both the boys' and the girls' sections, and there was never ever any animosity shown towards Jewish children by the teachers or by the other children in St Catherine's.

Jewish children from my neighbourhood also attended other schools. One of these was Donore School on the South Circular Road. Another was St Peter's in Bride Street, which was a boys' school. The headmaster of St Peter's was the well-known Mr Sleet, who had the reputation of being very strict. A number of Jewish boys, including my eldest brother Sam, went to the Kildare Place School in Kildare Street. The Damer School on St Stephen's Green also had Jewish pupils, and some of the boys were sent to St Andrew's and High School.

Many of the students from St Peter's and from the Damer School obtained scholarships to Wesley College, which was a mixed school. Jewish pupils also attended a junior school in Grosvenor Road, Rathgar. Many of the girls obtained scholarships from this school to Alexandra College in Earlsfort Terrace, and a number went on from there to gain recognition in public life. From all this it is evident that there were never any restrictions on Jewish children attending Catholic or Protestant schools in Dublin or other parts of Ireland. This also applied to the universities.

When school ended at 2.30 pm, we had a light meal and then I went to Hebrew class with my brother Harry for nearly two hours. Rabbi Gavron was our teacher and he was helped by his daughters Becky and Lily. Every week the Rabbi or his daughter would go through the *Siddur* (the daily and Sabbath prayer book) page by page, so that we knew what had to be said on each day and on festivals. When any boy was preparing for his *Bar Mitzvah*, around his thirteenth birthday, all the other pupils would take part and learn the *trops* or *nigin* (notes). Very few would ever forget these notes handed down over thousands of years.

I was very happy with Rabbi Gavron, but then my mother (it was always my mother who made the decisions) moved me to the *Talmud Torah* (Hebrew school). Jack Weingreen was our teacher. He was an extremely nice man, but a timid teacher who could not control the class. There was a boy called Stein who really got me into trouble one day. We were both sent to Mr Vilensky the headmaster. Without asking any questions about what had happened, he told Harry Stein to hold out his hand. Down came the long cane with great force. This was repeated twice on each hand. When it came to my turn, I put out my hand and as the cane came down I ran out of the room, never to return to the school. I had been there for only about six months. I was then sent to a teacher called Rev. Chiat who lived in Victoria Street. He had only three pupils: Hyman and Ivor Noyek and myself.

I know that my mother would have been very proud to know that I could be called up at any time in the synagogue to recite the *Haftorah* on the Saturday or on any festival, even without prior notice. I know that this is the result of her persistence in sending me to private Hebrew teachers. When I think of this, I know that there was love there. My parents spent a lot of money on my Hebrew education.

When homework and Hebrew class were over we had plenty of time for play, especially in the spring or late summer. We made our own fun. We used to play all kinds of games in the street, because there were no playgrounds in the area. It was normal for boys and girls to play together. I am referring to Jewish and non-Jewish children. Skipping and rounders were quite popular. Even the girls would join in when we played with marbles. Naturally, football was the most popular game with the boys. But we had to keep a sharp lookout for the police who toured around on bicycles. When a policeman was seen, we would either run indoors or hide wherever we could because it was against the law to play football in the street.

But there was one Jewish boy who didn't get away in time. When the policeman asked him for his name, he replied (with a pronounced stutter) 'B-B-B-Byrne'. This was not exactly a Jewish name, but had evidently been changed from another one that was hard to pronounce or spell. Then the policeman asked the boy for his Christian name, and he said 'I-I-I- haven't got a Christian name. I am a Jew.' The boy, who was only eight years old, got off with a caution. That incident did not stop us playing football; we just took more care.

On another occasion, when we were playing football in the street, I was not quick enough to get away and was caught by a policeman. I had to go to Court. My mother brought me there, as you had to have a parent with you. The Judge looked at me and gave me a stern warning about the dangers of playing football in the street. I was fined one shilling which my mother paid. I was convinced that I could see a glint in the Judge's eye when he was telling me not to play on the street any more.

In the evening, a group of us would be chatting together on the street and wondering what to do to pass the time. We would also be waiting for a Mr Lynch who lived across the road from our house. He usually walked past us, but sometimes if he had drink on him he would toss up a handful of pennies and ha'pennies right in front of us. No doubt, he enjoyed watching us scrambling for the coins. This happened quite often, and I'm glad to say that I always managed to pick up a few pennies.

Eddy Cartwright, Hugh Keogh and, of course, John Kelly were close friends of mine. They were non-Jewish boys who lived in Greenville Terrace, and we always went around together. When I see blackberries nowadays, I remember how often I went with John,

Eddy and Hugh to pick blackberries in Crumlin, which was an area of open fields at that time. We also used to collect chestnuts together. We had to walk about two miles since we had no money for tram fares, but that didn't bother us. We would find heavy sticks to knock down the chestnuts that we then brought home in our pockets. They were used to play conkers, a game that could be fiercely competitive.

Another of our games was called 'boxing the fox'. This was a great favourite with the boys. A group of us, maybe four or five, would get over a wall into a back garden where we knew there were ripe apples or pears. One of us would climb up the tree and throw down the fruit to be shared later. Sometimes we would be chased, and this only added to the excitement. On one occasion I was up a very large pear tree, throwing down the pears, when one of the boys shouted 'run' because the owner was coming out. I stayed where I was, because I knew that I wouldn't be able to get down and away in time. I also knew that the man couldn't see me because the tree was large and leafy. After he went back into the house, I waited for at least fifteen minutes before getting down with pockets full of pears.

Many years later, some of these exciting moments came back to me. There is a very big chestnut tree in the back garden of the house where Riv and I have lived for more than thirty years. One Saturday when I came back from synagogue and was sitting down to eat, Riv said 'Look, there are three boys in the garden throwing sticks up at the chestnut tree.' When I looked out and saw the children, my mind went back to the time when I was their age and was doing the same thing. So, I said, 'Just leave them and let's finish our meal.'

When I opened the back door quietly and went out, two of the boys saw me, ran out through the hedge and got over the fence into the field at the back of the garden, but the third boy was only about seven years old and couldn't get away quickly enough. I told him not to run away and asked him if he got any chestnuts. He replied

'No'. So I told him that I didn't mind them trying to knock down chestnuts, and offered to help him. 'Let's try together,' I said, 'I have some big sticks.' We were really enjoying ourselves when I began to wonder where the other two boys had got to. Just then, I saw two small faces appearing from behind a bush. I told them to come in, and for the next hour or more I had a wonderful time with those three children. I gave them lemonade and biscuits, which I never got at their age. They went away with bags of chestnuts. They did not have very far to go because all of them lived in the neighbourhood.

We used to go the local picture house in Camden Street to see Hoot Gibson, a cowboy film star, or Tom Mix and his horse Silver. These were serials and there would be a new episode every week. We had to save our pennies. It cost four pence to get in, but it was good value because the programme was continuous and we could see it from beginning to end two or thee times for our four pence. I still remember some of the films that we enjoyed so much. They would always end at a very exciting point, to make sure that we came back the next week.

Boys enjoyed saving cigarette cards. These cards were included in every box of cigarettes sold. Each one had a picture on one side and an explanatory note on the other side. The pictures would show various scenes or people. I used to collect cards of footballers and try to make up a set by swapping with other boys. These sets of picture cards are now fetching hundreds of pounds at auctions. Unfortunately, I never saved the cards.

During the summer a few of us would go to Seapoint for a swim. We had to go to Westland Row station to get a train there. There were two enclosed swimming pools in Dublin at the time, but we wanted to bathe in seawater so we went to Seapoint. When the tide was in it came right up to the rocks, where we would just strip off and walk into the water. None of us could swim then, so we splashed about and lowered ourselves into the water to give the impression that we were swimming. After going to Seapoint several times I plucked up courage, lifted my feet off the sand and did the breast stroke. Swimming was enjoyable from then on, and we were able to boast that we could swim out of our depth.

I remember an amusing incident at Seapoint Station while we were waiting for the train. It was a small station and some children were running about on the narrow platform, while their mothers chatted to each other. As the train was coming around the bend approaching the station, I heard one of the women shouting to her son 'Johnny, if you run under that train I'll murder you!'

Years later when I had a bicycle, a friend and I would cycle out to Seapoint for a swim after work. Sometimes, when the tide was out, we would have to walk several hundred yards to reach the water's edge. But it never bothered us, as we had nowhere else to go. My mother usually knew I had gone for a swim if I was not home by a certain time after work. I had that bicycle for years and I took great care of it. I enjoyed being able to go to so many places with it, and I had it for many years after I got married.

In the late 1920s I joined 'Woodcraft' which was like the Boy Scouts. At that time there was no Jewish Boy Scouts organisation; that came much later. The 'Woodcraft' leaders were Jack Segal and Leslie Yodaiken, and we met in the basement of Adelaide Road Synagogue once a week. Bernie Freeman and I became friends and we would always do things together. We learned many strange songs and we were taught how to make knots in ropes. We also went on long walks up the mountains. The Pine Forest was the area we liked best. We always brought food with us and Bernie and I would make the fire with twigs and pieces of wood. It was very exciting and very challenging. We were always on the look out for adventure.

We often went to Blackrock Baths, and now that I had become a fairly good swimmer I was able to swim at the deep end of the pool. Bernie was an excellent swimmer and I envied his ability to do the crawl stroke. He was also very good at diving, and would go off the top diving board which was about twenty feet high. I never had the nerve to dive from heights. Bernie also had a bicycle and I would sit on the crossbar while he raced around corners. We lived dangerously!

There are a lot of good memories, but there was also one very sad event when I was growing up in Greenville Terrace. This was the death of John Kelly, one of my best friends. He was around my age, twelve or thirteen at the time. He was taken to hospital one day, and I remember calling to his house which was about six doors from ours. His sister knew that we were close friends. She told me that John had TB and was seriously ill, but it came as a big shock when I heard that he had died. I was heartbroken, because we were real pals. I went to his funeral with Eddie Cartwright and Hugh Keogh. He was buried in Mount Jerome near Harold's Cross. We were told that TB was widespread in the country and was causing many deaths; it was a long time before it was brought under control.

In all the years living in Greenville Terrace I don't remember any unpleasantness between our non-Jewish neighbours and ourselves. It was the same in St Catherine's School. While there was plenty of friendly competition, we all got on well together. I can recall only one fight there and that was with a Jewish boy called Morris Rummel. I don't remember the reason for the fight, but within a week or two we were friends again. Morris now lives in Rathfarnham and I still see him occasionally in Terenure Synagogue. When I reminded him that we had a fight when we were at school, he didn't remember it but he asked who won.

Towards the end of the 1920s, the Corporation began to build houses in The Tenters, the large field at the end of Greenville Terrace. Before the building work began we used to play football and other games in the field, but we sometimes felt uneasy about what seemed to be a rough group of boys coming from the field and walking up our street to get to the South Circular Road. We tended to ignore them, but one day when I was talking to a Jewish friend, three boys from The Tenters stopped in front of us and one of them said 'You're a Jewman aren't you?' It was the first time I had heard anyone using that expression. When I did not reply, he then said 'You killed Christ.'

After I recovered from this attack, I said 'If you are looking for a fight, I am not afraid of you.' By then a number of boys and girls had gathered around us and, seeing my friends there, I began to feel better. He agreed to fight me and we walked back to The Tenters. As the word went around that there was going to be a fight, more people gathered and they formed a circle with the two of us in the middle. The fight stopped when my opponent got a black eye from one of my punches. Another fight with a boy from that area was with Alec Jordan who later came to work for me and became the foreman presser in the factory.

I was never a bully and I never looked for trouble, but being Jewish seemed to make me a target for some people. Some time after the fight in The Tenters, there was another incident of this kind. I was coming home from school in Westland Row. I noticed that three boys on the bus kept looking at me and appeared to be talking about me. When the bus stopped at my street I got out and crossed the road, followed by the same three boys. I knew there was trouble ahead.

At the top of Greenville Terrace there was a wall. Suddenly I was hemmed in against the wall, and they started with the same taunt: 'You are a Jewman.' I replied 'What of it? I'm not afraid of any of you.' With that one of them caught hold of my school bag and I hit him hard with a punch that made his nose bleed. I also punched one of the other two, and the fight was over. I did not feel elated at being able to defend myself. I was concerned about what would happen if they attacked a Jewish boy who could not defend himself, and I knew there were many of them.

# 5 Festivals, Rituals and Rites of Passage

From an early age I sang in the synagogue choir, and I have a clear memory of the preparations for the opening service in the newly built Greenville Hall in 1925. The choirmaster was Leo Bryll. It was a Friday night and the synagogue was filled to capacity. There were even chairs placed in the aisles. The atmosphere was very tense and there was a steady buzz as people chatted to each other. The choir stood waiting, all tensed up, as this was the first time that they were singing at a service.

Suddenly, there was silence. The doors opened and Cantor Rosenfield entered. He moved forward, singing *Ma Tovu*, the opening prayer on entering the Synagogue, and then the choir joined in. I was only a young boy, but I can still remember the shiver that ran through me at that time. As the service continued, the choirmaster sang a solo in his magnificent baritone voice. It was an unforgettable occasion, and I can still remember the joy and excitement of it all.

I remember seeing men like Bera Levy, Abraham Jackson and Reuben Segal in the Greenville Hall *shul* when I was a boy about ten years old, and to me they were very impressive and very old men. I remember watching them conferring with each other during the service, and they gave me a warm feeling of confidence and security, knowing that the community was in safe hands.

Issy Rosen and Teddy Lewis were in the choir with me. I single them out after so many years because they had such splendid voices and often thrilled the congregants with beautiful duets. Issy qualified as a doctor and emigrated to England. Teddy Lewis became a Rabbi. After some time in Dublin, he became the Rabbi of the Truro

Synagogue in Newport, Rhode Island, the oldest synagogue in the United States. Whenever he returned to Dublin on a visit I was very happy to meet him either at Adelaide Road Synagogue or in Terenure Synagogue. His face used to light up when he saw me, as we had grown up together.

I must put down the names of some of the older members of the choir also. Starting from the left, I remember Hyman Lazarus and Joe Cristol singing bass. Barney Rubenstein, Sam Jacobs and Maurice Davis were tenors. Mr Carroll and Mr Platt were baritones. Dave Green and Phil Rubenstein also sang with us. There were at least seven sopranos and an equal number of altos in the choir. Later, when I joined the choir in Adelaide Road, I sang as a tenor.

I sang in the choir in the Greenville *shul* for many years. I remember a time when each of the boys was given a pocket watch. What the adult members were given I do not remember. We were also supposed to receive a half crown per month. After about two months there was no more money, but we still enjoyed singing in the choir. Neither the boys nor the grown ups were ever taught to read music, and long afterwards I used to wonder how the choirmaster managed to teach us such wonderful pieces, some of which I still remember.

Every Saturday during the reading of the *Torah* (the five Books of Moses) the choir would go to a nearby house where the Marcus family lived. There we had tea, fairy cakes, cinnamon rolls and fruit slices, and we always looked forward to this. In the 1920s the service began at 8 am and usually finished at 1 pm. Now the Sabbath service in Dublin and in England starts at 9.15 am and finishes before noon.

One of my lasting memories of Greenville Hall Synagogue was when I was very young, but to this day I have never forgotten it. When the *Shabbos* service was over, members of the synagogue would pass by Rabbi Herzog, shake his hand and wish him 'Good *Shabbos*'. On one such occasion I was behind a man whom I knew as a Mr Cowan. He was a dentist and had a disability, having one leg shorter than the other, and wore a big boot to compensate. He was talking to the Rabbi and wished him good *Shabbos*. I then heard him say, 'Rabbi, is it a sin for me to take the tram to *shul*?' (It was desecrating the *Shabbos* to use transport on that day.) The Rabbi's reply was instantaneous. 'Mr Cowan,' he said, 'it is always a pleasure to see you in *shul* on *Shabbos*'. It was such a wonderful reply, I thought, of tact and understanding, and I never forgot it.

*Purim* was the first festival we celebrated in the year. It was a time for rejoicing. We would go to the Synagogue to listen to the *Megillah* (the story of Esther). The *Megillah* is read in synagogues all over the world during *Purim*. Esther, the beautiful Queen of Persia, was Jewish. She persuaded King Ahasuerus to prevent Haman, his Prime Minister, from carrying out a plan to slaughter all the Jews in Persia. The Jews were saved and Haman ended up being executed instead. *Purim* commemorates the rescue of the Jews of Persia from Haman's plot to exterminate them.

The Rabbi unrolls the scroll and starts to read. Whenever Haman is mentioned, the children bang their feet on the floor. We used to have *dradles* or rattles which made a loud noise when we twisted them around. In my day, many of the children took the opportunity to wear fancy dress and we would feast on the *hamantashen* made by our mothers. These were three-cornered cakes filled with poppy seeds and honey and they were delicious to eat. The *hamantashen* were made with three corners because we believed that Haman always wore a three-cornered hat. Everybody enjoyed the festival of *Purim*, because the story had such a happy ending.

As soon as *Purim* was over, our parents began preparing for *Pesach* which was only a month away. My mother would order a box of one hundred eggs and received an extra twenty, but it was always referred to as a box of one hundred. Eggs were used extensively at *Pesach*. Nearly all the food we ate had eggs in it: eggs for the *Seder* nights (the first two nights of Passover), eggs for the sponge cakes, eggs for the *matzo* balls in the soup.

*Pesach* was the second festival in the year, and it was the one I most looked forward to. A week before *Pesach*, my father and mother made a drink they called 'mead', which was made from hops, like beer, and sweeetened with honey or sugar. There was so much preparation. Everything had to be washed and *kosher*ed. All the *chomatz* (anything that was not *kosher* for *Pesach*) had to be cleared away. I remember my father searching for the *chomatz* that had been left out the night before. He took it up with two or more long feathers and gathered it together. Then I was told to bring the *chomatz* to the Rabbi. This is what is termed 'selling the *chomatz*', an old tradition still carried on by Orthodox Jews. The Rabbi would give the money to charity. During the week of Passover it was forbidden to use toothpaste as it was regarded as *chomatz*, and we had to use salt instead. Now we can get all kinds of Passover needs.

The gas cooker had to be scrubbed and covered. The delph used during the year was put away, and the pots and pans and delph for *Pesach* were taken out, put on the dresser and covered with a white sheet. I can remember that the cutlery was stuck into the earth in the garden, left there for a few days and then washed. There was a lot to be done, and my mother and eldest sister Leah worked very hard preparing for the *Seder* nights. It was the time when families got together; a time when parents carried on customs and traditions they had seen in their own homes; the time when the boys got new suits and girls got new dresses; a time of happy memories.

The festival of *Pesach* lasts for eight days, and we were always told that it is a very important festival for Jewish children. The *Haggadah* (narrative read aloud at the Passover *Seder*) is read on the *Seder* nights. The grandfather, father or eldest son makes the blessing of the *kosher* wine. The youngest boy asks four questions about the meaning of the Passover, starting with the question 'Why is this night different from all other nights of the year?' Responses to the questions come in the reading of *Haggadah* which tells the story of the Exodus of the people of Israel from slavery in Egypt, the ten plagues in Egypt, the crossing of the Red Sea, the parting of the waves that let them through while swallowing up the Egyptians and their chariots, their forty years in the wilderness before coming into the promised land. The *Seder* always concludes with the words 'Next year may we be in Israel.' During the reading of the *Haggadah* four glasses of wine are consumed.

Our *Seder* nights were full of symbolism and singing and the reading of the *Haggadah*. We listened as my father read the same story that is repeated every year on those first two nights of Passover, and then it was time for the specially prepared food, including the *matzo* (unleavened Passover bread) which tasted wonderful. I remember a Passover during World War II when we had to celebrate without *matzo* because the necessary supplies did not arrive from England. However, we had a substitute *matzo* which was baked in a factory in Dublin under the supervision of Mr Steinberg, the 'salt king' of Ireland. He persuaded Spratts, a company that manufactured dog biscuits, to make one of their ovens available to bake *matzos* for the Jewish community.

Mr Steinberg, who was very orthodox, undertook to supervise the whole operation, and there is no doubt that Spratts' ovens were thoroughly cleaned and made *kosher* to bake the *matzos*. But, unfortunately, what came out of the ovens was like dog biscuits, thick and hard as a rock, and had to be soaked in water for at least two days before you could attempt to eat it. Even if the results did not come up to expectations, Mr Steinberg deserved congratulations for his efforts to provide the community with the genuine article, and Spratts deserved our gratitude for allowing their ovens to be used. It is the only *Pesach* I remember when we had no proper *matzo*.

For some time after World War II it was also impossible to get *kosher* sweets for *Pesach*. Recently, I was told an interesting story about how the problem was overcome on one occasion in the 1950s. Freda Jacks, who worked in Lemon's Sweets factory in Drumcondra for over twenty years, told me what happened. Coming up to *Pesach*, there were still no sweets available. On his own initiative, Rabbi Alony went to Lemon's and spoke to the owner, a Mr Tate. He told him about the festival of Passover, and explained that the Jewish people—especially the children—were deprived of sweets for the festival period unless the sweets conformed to the *kosher* regulations for Passover.

After a brief discussion, Mr Tate agreed to allow Rabbi Alony to use one of the factory vats to manufacture boiled sweets. With the assistance of two of the staff, the Rabbi thoroughly cleaned and washed the selected vat to prepare it for producing the sweets. Freda Jacks was able to see what was going on. She remembers that some of the staff resented the way the vat was being prepared. They said 'The Rabbi must think we are not clean,' until Freda informed them of the reason for the strict preparation.

The Rabbi was present at all times while the sweets were being manufactured, and in the evening a seal was put on the vat to secure it overnight. After a few days there was a sufficient quantity of sweets ready to meet the needs of the community. I don't know if any payment was made to Lemon's Sweets, but I do know that Rabbi Alony supplied all the ingredients. Rabbi Alony was congratulated on his enterprise and Mr Tate deserved the thanks of the community for allowing his premises to be used.

It was usual to invite people to the *Seder* who would otherwise be on their own, and on many occasions we had people to join us. When we finished our *Seder*, usually after eleven o'clock, some of the boys would go to Steinberg's house on the South Circular Road to listen to the arguments and the questions that arose from passages in the *Haggadah*. Their service went on until well after midnight. On the first two days of Passover, we would go to the synagogue service that usually started at eight o'clock in the morning.

*Rosh Hashanah* (the Jewish New Year) seemed to come very quickly after *Pesach*. It was a holiday we enjoyed very much: two days of endless eating and holidays from school. Then came *Yom Kippur* (the Day of Atonement) when a total fast was observed. *Rosh Hashanah* and *Yom Kippur* are the most important festivals, and are celebrated on the same days all over the world wherever there are Jewish people. *Rosh Hashanah* is a religious festival, not like Passover or *Chanukah* (the Feast of Lights). It is about prayer, and tradition tells us that on *Rosh Hashanah* God judges his people. The ten days between *Rosh Hashanah* and *Yom Kippur* are called the Ten Days of Penitence, and they allow the people to repent for wrongs committed during the year. On *Yom Kippur* all Jews over the age of thirteen are obliged to fast and repent and to pray that they may be better people during the coming year.

Many of the older members of the community and those whose parents were very orthodox will remember the ritual that was observed on the morning before the fast of *Yom Kippur*. This was the ceremony known as *shlogn kapores*, and was carried out in the home by the fathers and the boys before going to work or to school. When I was very young I was shown what to do. If possible a live white-feathered hen was used to perform the ceremony. You held the hen in your hands, raised it over your head, circled it three times around your head, and said a prayer. Then my mother would give me a small amount of money to place in a special collection box to help the *Yeshiva* (school for potential Rabbis).

In this special ceremony the hen became a scapegoat, and your sins were transferred to the hen. When all the male members of the family had performed the ceremony, one of the boys would bring the hen to the abattoir to be killed. The hen was then used for a meal before the fast began. In later years when people no longer kept hens, money was used to perform the ceremony. I doubt if this ritual is continued in many Jewish families today.

*Yom Kippur* was followed by *Succoth*, the harvest festival called the Feast of Booths (or Tabernacles). For this thanksgiving festival, the ladies' committee decorated the synagogue. The *succah* or booth represents the temporary dwellings in which the people lived in the fields during the harvest. It also represents the hastily set-up dwellings which the Jews used during their forty years in the wilderness.

*Succoth* is held at the time of ingathering of the harvest in ancient Palestine. The festival lasts for a week. Special prayers were said each day, and in every synagogue there was a *lulav* and *ethrog*. The *lulav* is made with palm leaves tied together with twigs of myrtle and branches of willow. The *ethrog* is a special citrus fruit from a tree of the orange and lemon family. The beadle of the synagogue would bring the *lulav* and *ethrog* to every member of the synagogue, and each one would recite a special prayer.

Few members of synagogues in Dublin in the 1920s and 1930s could afford a *lulav* and *ethrog* of their own. Because of their work, many of them could not attend the synagogue during the week. But they all wanted to say the special blessing, so the *lulav* and *ethrog* were brought to them in their homes. Rabbi Gavron, my Hebrew teacher, selected me to bring the *lulav* and *ethrog* to the people in my area. There would have been more than thirty houses. I called to each of them before I went to school in the morning. At the end, I received sixpence from each house, and many people gave me a shilling. I am not sure if this was before or after my *Bar Mitzvah*, but I know I was still attending Rabbi Gavron's *cheder* (Hebrew school) at the time.

On the final day of *Succoth* we celebrated *Simchath Torah*, when the men sang and danced as they carried the *Sefer Torah* (scroll containing the five Books of Moses) around the synagogue. This is the end of the festival of *Succoth*. The last portion of the five books of Moses is read out, and then the first book of the *Torah* is read, so that the continuous reading of the *Torah* never ends. The children were not left out. We gathered around the *bema* (pulpit) and chanted the prayer. Then we were given bags of sweets, and if you were smart you could get more than one bag. I have to say that I was one of the smart boys and did very well. On *Simchath Torah* the festivities went on all day. Many boys and girls went to the Chief Rabbi's home to continue the celebrations into the night. Years later, I used to supply the sweets for this occasion myself.

When I had my *Bar Mitzvah* there was no party. The Rabbi and a number of men came back to the house for a *Kiddush* and then helped themselves to what had been prepared by my mother and my sister Leah. I must have received presents, but I cannot remember getting them. I got a *talith* (prayer shawl) and *tefillin* (phylacteries), and I remember clearly getting five shillings from Sam Farbenbloom. Sam, who came from Czechoslovakia, had married my sister Leah. When we were young we would go to *shul* every week. After my *Bar Mitzvah* we would regularly attend services on Friday night and in the morning and afternoon on Saturday.

In the 1930s most Jewish weddings were celebrated in the Greenville Hall at the back of the synagogue. The *chuppa* (the word means wedding canopy but is often used to signify the wedding ceremony) would usually be at 2 pm and the dinner would be timed for some time after 4 pm. Annie Danker was responsible for the catering at many of these weddings and the food she served is still talked about in the community. The tables were all decorated with fresh flowers and an array of fruits. The meal started with an exotic first course. Then there was Annie's famous chicken soup with *kreplach* (dumplings), *lockshen* (noodles, vermicelli) and *perogen* (minced meat rolls). This was followed by chicken, turkey or cold meat, then fresh vegetables; then various kinds of fresh fruit; then a selection of desserts and *pareveh* ice cream (made without milk solids or butter fat); and finally coffee or lemon tea. At the end of the meal the bride's father would offer cigars to the men.

When dinner was over the tables were cleared for dancing. I can remember the mothers sitting on both sides of the Hall watching the young people dancing, and nodding and whispering to each other about the prospects of those girls and boys for a *shiddach* (a good match). The men would retire to an upstairs room in the caretaker's house for cards. Solo and poker were popular, and after about two and a half hours there would be an interval when tea and pastries were served. Annie Danker's moment of glory was when she came out from the kitchen wearing her pinafore and slippers, and walked around the dance floor carrying a tray of assorted chocolates. She beamed with pleasure as she acknowledged compliments and praise from every one of the guests.

At about 10 pm the waitresses went around with cups of chicken soup, platters of pickled meat and tongue sandwiches. The card players received special attention, because the waitresses knew that they would get a handsome tip from them. When Annie died her sister Bloomy carried on with the catering in more or less the same way, but there will never be another Annie Danker.

Few people had cars in those days. Mr Mirrelson lived in Dufferin Avenue and had a fleet of four Chrysler cars imported from America. Whenever there was a Jewish wedding his cars were in operation all day, ferrying people to the synagogue for the ceremony and reception and bringing them back to their homes later. It was usual to have one or two groomsmen in charge of organising the cars to collect various people. If two couples were being collected in a particular car, the groomsmen had to make sure that they were friends. The groomsmen also had to ensure that the close members of the family were not brought to the synagogue too early. Some people demanded to be called for even though they lived only a short distance away.

I can tell you it was a headache coping with all these arrangements, especially when you called at a house and you had to wait. All the guests who were to be collected were informed as to the time the car would arrive. If you think it was the women who were not ready, you would be wrong. In most cases it was the men, and their excuse was that they couldn't get away from a meeting. I was a groomsman at several weddings. There were always some people who behaved as if they were the only ones being called for. And then, when you had nearly all the guests collected, you had to send the best car for the Rabbi and his wife, and make sure that he did not arrive too early. This was a service that the bride's family had to provide.

There are three requirements for a Jewish community: a synagogue, a *mikvah* (ritual bath) and a burial ground. Men and women go to the synagogue to pray and also to take part in the normal community activities. The *mikvah* is a pool that would hold approximately 200 gallons of natural rainwater and is used by religious people, men and women. It is customary for men to go to the *mikvah* every Friday before the *Shabbos*, and for women to go every month.

The first Jewish burial ground in Dublin was opened in 1777 in Ballybough, near Fairview on the north side of the city. By 1889 the growing community needed a larger cemetery on the south side, and the committee of the *Chevra Kaddishah* (Holy Burial Society) purchased the plot of ground that is now the cemetery at Dolphin's Barn. Before Rabbi Alony left Dublin to take up a position in the Beth Din in London he was heard to say that the *Chevra Kaddishah* in Dublin was a unique institution, in that no member of it received payment of any kind. The only person to receive any payment in connection with a funeral in Dolphin's Barn is the caretaker who lives next to the cemetery.

The members of the Burial Society are people from many walks of life, including doctors, dentists, business people. They are selfless men and women honouring an ancient tradition with no thought of reward. Going back many years, I remember Louis Levinson, Aaron Steinberg and his son Louis, Sid Cole, Abraham Elzas, Willy Stein, Willy Zeider and many others whose names I can't recall. Today's members include Solly Rhodes, Terry Samuels, Seton Menton, Cecil Calmonson, Jeffrey Garber, Adrian Gordon, David Ross, Alan Miller, Howard Gross and Edward Segal. Members of the ladies' committee are Mrs B. Feldman, Mrs M. Gordon, Mrs H. Gross, Mrs L. Levine, Mrs A. Lewis, Mrs E. Menton, Mrs M. Miller and Mrs R. Stein.

Every Jewish person who dies has the same status as any other and there is no distinction as to position or rank. Be they housewife, Rabbi, judge or carpenter, each one is buried in a plain unadorned wooden coffin. If the death takes place in hospital, members of the medical or nursing staff are asked not to touch the body. Regardless of the time of day or night, a phone call is made to the *gabbai* (contact person) of the Burial Society. Members of the Burial Society arrive and a whole routine is set in motion.

If a man has died, male members of Burial Society come to the hospital or to the family home. If the deceased is a woman, lady members come. The first thing they do is to wrap the body in a sheet and place it on the floor, where it stays until the coffin arrives. It is customary that a member of the family or a friend or a person appointed by the Burial Society would stay with body until it is placed in the coffin. It is then brought to the mortuary where it is washed by the same members of the Burial Society.

If the body is that of a man, it is dressed in a pair of white linen trousers and jacket, and a white cap is placed on the head. A garment with fringes on both sides is put over the jacket and another jacket is put over that. Then a *talith* (prayer shawl) that is normally worn by a male in the synagogue is put around the upper part of the body. Finally, the body is completely covered with a sheet. The body of a woman is put in white linen garments but without the fringes or the *talith*, because Orthodox women do not wear a *talith* in the synagogue. Earth brought from Israel is sprinkled three times over the body.

The coffin is closed and brought to the prayer house. The Cantor intones the prayer for the dead before it is brought out into the graveyard by members of the Burial Society, followed by the Cantor chanting passages of the funeral service. Members of the Burial Society lower the coffin into the grave and begin to fill it in. Family members are given a spade and each adds three shovels full of earth. Friends of the deceased do likewise until the grave has been completely filled in. The Cantor then recites the burial service and the male members of the family say the *Kaddish* (prayer for the dead).

After the burial the family members return to the prayer house. People file by offering sympathy and wishing them 'long life'. A member of the Burial Society announces where the *shivah* (seven solemn days of mourning) will take place and the times for prayers to be said in the *shivah* house. When the mourners return home, they are offered the traditional bagels and hard-boiled eggs prepared by close friends. Burial Society members would have already brought prayer books and the stools for the mourners to sit on. Ten men (a *minyan*) have to be present for the prayers that are said two or three times on each of the seven days. Relatives and friends provide all the meals for the family during the seven days, and visitors are not offered any food while the mourners are sitting *shivah*.

From the moment the *gabbai* is informed of a death, all the arrangements are taken over by the Burial Society. This service is provided for all members of the Jewish community who are members of the synagogue and contribute to the Burial Society. In many cases the members of the Holy Burial Society would go out of their way, if they heard of a Jewish person who was a stranger to the community, to bury that person in the Jewish cemetery. It was considered a duty to do so, even if no payment is made. Jews who are not members of a synagogue are entitled to be buried in the Jewish cemetery with exactly the same funeral rites, but in this case the family is expected to make a contribution to the cost, according to their means. I had experience of this situation when my brother Harry died.

I was called to the mortuary in the burial grounds where his body lay in an open coffin. I was asked to put a white skullcap on his head and recite a special prayer. Then a member of the burial society made a cut on the right side of the waistcoat that I was wearing. This is an ancient tradition. For a mother or father, the cut would be on the left side.

Harry had married out and was never a member of a synagogue. Before he died his wife told me that he had expressed a wish to be buried in the Jewish cemetery. This surprised me as Harry had never shown any inclination to be involved in the affairs of the Jewish community, but I was pleased to know that he had not forgotten his Jewish roots. I told his wife that since he was never a member of a synagogue it might be expensive to be buried in the Jewish cemetery, but she was willing to make whatever payment was required. Harry's funeral in Dolphin's Barn was attended by his wife, daughter, son-in-law and a number of non-Jewish friends. They were very impressed by the dignity of the service. I said the *Kaddish* for my brother, I continued to say the *Kaddish* for thirty days in accordance with Jewish tradition, and I will continue to say *Kaddish* on the anniversary of his death every year.

# 6 Spreading My Wings

When I was nearly fourteen my parents enrolled me in a Catholic school at Westland Row. Except for a few, all the teachers were Christian Brothers. The teaching was on a much higher level than at St Catherine's. The school had an excellent record, and many of the boys became civil servants. There were only three Jewish boys among about two hundred pupils. In my class of around thirty there were two other Jewish boys, Cecil Fridjohn and Izzy Leventhal. The three of us got on very well with our classmates and I settled down quickly. The Brothers were strict and the leather strap was used, but I was never punished and neither were the other Jewish boys.

To get from Greenville Terrace to Westland Row School, I took a bus on the South Circular Road that left me just outside the school. This was a private bus service run by Andrew Clarkin. It was called the 'Carmel' bus. There was another service called the 'Blue Line' that competed with the 'Carmel' bus. At that time, there was no public bus service with regular stopping places, so the private buses just stopped anywhere to pick up passengers.

Some years later, I got to know Andrew Clarkin. He had various business interests. He was a coal merchant with a fleet of lorries; he also had a thriving tailoring business in Pearse Street, where I would often meet his wife and other members of his family when I was delivering men's suits. He was a charming man and had many Jewish friends. I was not at all surprised when he was chosen to serve as Lord Mayor of Dublin from 1952 to 1954.

Coming from such a religious background, I have no idea why I was sent to a Catholic school. I know my mother was not prejudiced and always had a good relationship with our neighbours who were mainly Catholics. But I never understood why I was sent to Westland Row, and I found it difficult to come to terms with this. Even after I left school and started work in the factory, my mother never told me why she had decided to send me there and it never struck me to ask.

The first indication I got of religious difference was when the clock struck twelve and the bells rang out in St Andrew's Church next to the school. Then the whole class, except for the three Jewish boys, knelt down on one knee and recited a prayer until the bells stopped ringing. While this was going on, we just sat in our seats and got on with our work. It was explained to me afterwards that the bells were ringing for the Angelus.

I can say truthfully that I got on well with most of my classmates in Westland Row, and also with some boys from other classes with whom I came in contact. John Geraghty and I were in the same class and became close friends. After leaving school we used to meet and go for long walks together. At weekends, one of our favourite places was along the banks of the river Dargle in Bray. To get there we would take the train from Harcourt Street station. We also enjoyed walking in Phoenix Park. Two years after we left school, John's parents decided to move to Canada and he had to go with them. We didn't keep in touch after that, but I have never forgotten him.

When I had been in Westland Row School for nearly a year, my parents got a letter from Leo Bryll, the former choirmaster at the Greenville Hall Synagogue. He had gone to Liverpool and was trying to form a choir in a *shul* there. He was anxious to get some former members of the Greenville Hall choir to go over for *Rosh Hashanah*, *Yom Kippur* and *Succoth*, three weeks in all. Several people had received letters but in the end only two went over, myself and Joe Cristol.

I brought the letter from Mr Bryll with me when I went to the head Brother in the school to ask for permission to go. He asked me a few questions about the festivals and then granted my request. I think he was pleased that a pupil from his school was selected for the choir. I remember that when I came back and handed up the homework I was given, I never heard anything about it, good or bad. I was away for nearly three weeks. Joe Cristol and I stayed in a Jewish boarding house, and it was my first holiday away from home. When we had our first rehearsal with the choir there we were not surprised that Mr Bryll wanted us to help out. They had difficulty in learning the songs. Joe and I were given many solos and duets to sing, and all in all it was a very good experience.

Joe Cristol was one of the most likeable characters in Dublin during my growing-up years. He was a great story-teller. I can still remember the stories he told to people in Liverpool when he and I were invited to meals in the homes of *shul* members. Each time he repeated a story it was embellished with more and more adventures, and as a young boy I was enthralled listening to him. When we moved to Victoria Street I saw much more of Joe. I don't remember if he had a job or what he worked at, but he was always to be seen around the street. He was at least ten years older that myself and my friends, but this didn't seem to matter when you were in his company. He was a very kind person, always in good humour, and I never heard a swear word from him. When the Progressive Synagogue opened in 1946, it gave Joe the opportunity to conduct the children's class and to be involved in organising the choir.

It was in Liverpool also that I was kissed by a girl for the first time. I became friendly with another choirboy called Nathie Restan, whose father owned a fish and chip restaurant. In between *Rosh Hashanah* and *Yom Kippur* we used to visit the restaurant and enjoy the chips and lemonade called 'Tizer' that his father gave us. One day Nathie invited me home for the mid-day meal and I met his two sisters. I remember that one of them was named Gertie. After the meal, one of the girls suggested playing 'spin the bottle'. Nathie and I were just over fourteen and the sisters were not much older. I had no idea what the game was about, as I had never played any game where girls were involved. But I soon found out when one of the girls spun the bottle and it stopped at herself. She leaned over and gave me a kiss. I was very embarrassed, but I recovered quickly and for the next hour or more I really enjoyed the game.

School holidays also provided opportunities to learn about the world of work at first hand. It was a coincidence that the house we moved to in Victoria Street was owned by Sam Yodaiken who lived in Leinster Road. Mr Yodaiken also owned the building in Ormond Quay where my father took the second floor for a factory employing over twenty men and women. This was near the end of the 1920s. I can remember that when we had school holidays I used to go there to bring my father the lunch that my mother prepared for him. I also remember being sent with some completed suits to Mr Ellis in his first floor shop in Henry Street. Mr Ellis would examine each garment to make sure it was perfect. He was a stern looking man and seldom smiled. I often thought I might get a small tip for bringing the suits to him, but I never got anything.

Another episode I remember from that time concerned two sewing machines that my father bought from a Mr Brennan who was a mechanic. The machines gave trouble right from the start. My father refused to pay for them, and Mr Brennan took him to Court. Father took me with him, as my brothers had to keep working. The judge decided in favour of Mr Brennan. Then he said 'Mr Brennan, I take it that you are an honourable man?' Mr Brennan replied that he was. The judge then said 'I would like you to take the two machines back from Mr Harris.' The case ended with Mr Brennan having to take back the two sewing machines.

Being in the factory during the school holidays made me realise how hard people had to work. Wages were small. I can remember one particular girl who was a trousers machinist, and a very fast worker. During a busy period she earned £1 12s for a week's work, a lot of money then. A girl's normal weekly wages would be between 15s and £1. They were all paid piece work, which meant they were paid for each garment they made. I do not know how those wages would compare with today, but I know people worked very hard.

Mr Bookbinder was a top presser. He had to use an iron (it was called a goose iron, I never knew why) that was heated by gas and was seven to ten pounds in weight. There was a frame in which two of these irons could be placed, and while one iron was being heated the finished garment was pressed with the other one. There were two frames, one for Mr Bookbinder and one for the other top presser. The under presser's job was to press open the seams of the garments. He had his own frame, but with lighter irons.

On the first floor of the building there was a Mr Lewis, an extremely nice man. He made ladies' coats and costumes. I can clearly remember watching some garments being made, and I saw one tailor putting tailoring soap on the front of coats — on the inside of course. When the garment was pressed, the front of the coat would be stuck to the facing. In fact, the same method was used by the tailors in my father's factory. The work was very demanding, and I know for a fact that Mr Lewis was paid 12s 6d for cutting, trimming and making a lady's coat. I still have an invoice for a two-piece suit that was made for a shopkeeper in Drogheda by my father. Mr Deeney paid £1 3s 9d for the suit, but he supplied the lining. Only those who lived during those years know how hard the clothing manufacturers had to work.

I also saw another aspect of work during the school holidays. One of my friends was Lionel Isaacson. His brother Dick had what was called a 'weekly business' and took us with him sometimes when he went to the country. I remember him stopping at different farms to collect payment for goods and to take further orders. It was a great day out for us, as Dick treated us to lunch in one of the towns we passed through. Sometimes we didn't return to Dublin until after nine o'clock in the evening.

Jewish people were comparatively poor in the early 1930s, although they were not short of the basic necessities. Most members of the community were in the same position. There was no money for luxuries. Very few people owned cars; some had a pony and trap to conduct their business. But the quality of life was rich. Most people had come from a common religious background, and there was a sense of togetherness in the community. It was only after some had achieved a certain level of affluence that divisions began to develop. But nobody looked down on people who were poor.

In those early years people turned to all kinds of work in order to make a living. I clearly remember a man who used to push a small cart with a large container fastened securely to it. The container held *kosher* oil that he sold to the Jewish housewives. Oil was used extensively for cooking. He had many customers for his oil and not too far to go. Another man pushed a small cart with a milk churn, and went from door to door selling milk. I think milk was four pence a pint at the time, and the milkman would also give you a 'tilly' (an extra portion). Sugar was four pence a pound and butter ten pence a pound. I am sure that many of my readers will remember the Monument Creamery shops owned by Mrs Ryan in various parts of the city. Many members of the Jewish community were regular customers for the dairy produce in those shops.

The 1930s were the years when parents scrimped and saved to give their sons a good education, especially if they had no business that their sons could go into. With regard to education all the attention was focused on the boys in the family. I can remember that many of the Jewish girls growing up in my time were much cleverer than their brothers, but they were expected to get positions as secretaries or salesgirls, to study music and, in time, to make a good *shiddach* (match/marriage).

After around three years with the Christian Brothers in Westland Row School, I went to work full time in my father's factory. After some years in the factory on Ormond Quay, my father and my eldest brother Sam negotiated a contract with the Fifty Shilling Tailors, an English company. They had a large shop on the corner of Cole's Lane and Henry Street. The contract was to produce at least three hundred suits per week. You had ten days to make the suits. Part of the contract was that the Fifty Shilling Tailors would update the factory with Hoffman pressing machines, special sewing machines, and many other features. They were prepared to set up a system to make the suits and sent in a consultant to do this. So a factory was leased in Smithfield and was set up by the English company. The contract also contained a clause that a certain amount of money would be deducted each week to pay for the equipment put in by the English company.

My first job was at the cutting table where three of us worked together: Mr Latham, a Yorkshire man, his son Jack, and myself. Mr Latham would mark each suit in chalk. Jack and I would cut out the suit and we had to be very quick. There was a target to be met. We had to work hard to meet this target, and we did meet it. I was at the cutting table for six months, and then moved to another area to get experience of how each garment was made. It was my own decision to go to the cutting table and then to other positions. I also learned to use every machine in the factory. My father did not direct any of his four sons working in the factory to any particular function. At the time I did not realise this, and I just went along on my own.

Next, I decided to look after the dispatch section, seeing to the delivery of the suits to the store of Fifty Shilling Tailors in Back Lane which runs parallel to High Street and Christchurch Place. I was responsible for checking the suit lengths in and for making sure that the finished garments were delivered on time. I also learned to use every machine in the factory. When I started work I was paid 2s 6d per week. I was able to walk to work and back, but later my mother gave me £2 to buy a bicycle, which was a great bonus. I was able to ride to and from work, and often went for a swim after work. I had that bicycle for many years and I took great care of it.

My pay of two shillings and six pence had to do me for the whole week. I was able to go to an Italian restaurant called Cafolla's, just off O'Connell Street, and for one shilling and three pence I could have fish (usually cod) and chips, tea, bread and butter, then go to the Savoy Cinema for one shilling, and have three pence over. If I got the tram home it cost two pence and I had a penny over. But if the weather was good I would walk home. For my shilling at the Savoy, I would see a full length film and a second feature film, a cartoon and the Pathe news. There was also an organ played by Tommy Dando. The full programme took about two and a half hours. After six months my wages were increased to ten shillings per week, due to my mother. This enabled me to save part of my wages each week for holidays and so on.

I was friendly with David Green who lived opposite our house, and we would often walk into town and go to the Savoy. When Tommy Dando played the organ he would invite the audience to join in and sing. Dave (who had a rich baritone voice) and I would sing out and heads would turn to see who the singers were. We would then go up to the restaurant to have tea and cake and listen to Joe van Aalst playing the violin and his wife playing the piano. They were excellent musicians and they occasionally played requests.

We also went to the Theatre Royal and to the Gaiety Theatre. The Theatre Royal was known for its first-class live show and for the orchestra led by Jimmy Campbell. In the Theatre Royal we saw Noel Purcell, Eddy Byrne and Mickser Reid. They were hilarious, particularly in a sketch with Noel dressed as a woman. Sometimes we saw international stars. There was also the troupe of dancers known as the Royalettes, trained by Alice Dalgarno and Babs del Monte. In the Gaiety Theatre we saw Jimmy O'Dea and Harry O'Donovan (who wrote all the scripts). They were great favourites with Dublin audiences.

It is almost impossible to think of theatre and cinema in Dublin during those years without remembering the Elliman family. When Maurice Elliman landed in Dublin in 1900 with little or no money he could not have foreseen the influence that he and his family were to have on the people of Ireland. He had come from Latvia to escape from the Tsarist regime. He was fortunate in his choice of Ireland as a place of safety and Ireland gained from his spirit of enterprise. His first business venture was a greengrocer's shop, but he had a vision about the motion picture industry which was then in its infancy. Where he obtained the equipment is not known. What is known is that he began his career in the motion picture business less than a year after his arrival in Dublin and never looked back.

He rented a room in Camden Street and showed films with a hand-operated projector on a makeshift screen erected on one of the walls. He usually had an audience of fifteen to twenty children who paid one penny each to see the movies. Corrigans, the undertakers, and Rourkes' Bakery, two of his neighbours in Camden Street, must have wondered what was going on when they saw boys and girls coming and going from Mr Elliman's premises. When they found out more about it they were very impressed and decided to invest in building a cinema with Maurice Elliman as manager. The Theatre de Luxe in Camden Street was Maurice Elliman's entry into the cinema business.

When he arrived in Dublin, Maurice lodged with the Smullen family. He married Leah Smullen and they had twelve children: nine boys and three girls. Hennie, the eldest daughter, married Henry White who was a ladies' clothing manufacturer. Queenie married Leslie Watson and Rose married Dr Copeland. With the exception of Hymie, who qualified as a doctor and moved to London, all the boys joined the company and were given positions in the cinemas as they grew up. Louis, the son who was to become the most prominent, was educated in Synge Street Christian Brothers School, a short distance from where he was born in Aungier Street. His father wanted him to be a chemist, and after qualification Louis worked for eight years in a chemist's shop in South Richmond Street. But his heart was in the film business, and when he reached the age of thirty he went to London where he contacted First National Films and became their agent.

When the Theatre Royal in Hawkins Street was demolished in 1934, Louis decided to rebuild it on the same site. In 1936 he advised his father to buy the Gaiety Theatre. By the late 1930s the Ellimans were firmly established in the theatre business as well as in the cinema business. In 1944 Louis joined the board of Irish Cinemas Ltd as director and vice-chairman under his father. The high point of his career was during the war years when Ireland was cut off from the rest of the entertainment world. Month after month the Theatre Royal provided cinema and variety shows.

Around 1945, the J. Arthur Rank organisation brought the various Elliman companies together under the title of Odeon (Ireland) Ltd and Louis became managing director, a post he held until he retired in 1963 for health reasons. When the Abbey Theatre was badly damaged by fire in 1951, Louis approached Ernest Blythe to offer the use of the nearby Queen's Theatre until the Abbey was rebuilt. The offer was accepted and Ernest Blythe was heard to say that Louis Elliman was really a friend in need. He was the driving force behind the establishment of Ardmore Studios in 1958, and this was certainly one of his outstanding achievements.

In 1962, when the Theatre Royal was sold and demolished to make way for an office block, Louis turned his attention to the Gaiety Theatre. He had a flair for the big spectacular type of show, but the spectacle always had to be laced with taste. Vulgarity in any form never found a place in his work. He supported the production of operas and plays in the Gaiety, but stayed in the background and left it to others to accept ovations from enthusiastic audiences. He was a very retiring person. He shunned publicity and was quick to give credit to everyone who helped him.

He was on very friendly terms with Count John McCormack and Margaret Burke Sheridan. Other close friends included Hilton Edwards, Michael Mac Liammóir, Jimmy O'Dea and Maureen Potter. It was Maureen who suggested, when Louis died, that the Gaiety should be renamed the Louis Elliman Theatre as a permanent memorial to this great and loveable man.

His funeral was attended by representatives of the theatre and cinema business as well as many other aspects of Irish life. The hearse was accompanied by a Garda escort. President de Valera was represented by Robert Briscoe TD, the Taoiseach was represented by his ADC, Commdt Jack O'Brien, and the Lord Mayor of Dublin represented the people of Dublin who always considered him as one of their own. Dayan Alony represented Chief Rabbi Cohen who was out of the country at the time.

Louis' funeral was one of the biggest ever to be held in Dolphin's Barn cemetery, and tributes continued to flow in for days. As they sat *shivah*, family members were able to reflect on the achievements of the Ellimans over fifty years of work that had left an indelible mark on cinema and theatre in Dublin.

When we were in our early twenties one of our recreations was playing snooker. From time to time a few of us would visit places where there were snooker tables, and the best known of these was the Cosmo in O'Connell Street. I used to go with Dave Green. We were only very average and our bet was that whoever lost would pay for the use of the table. Dave had twin brothers older than himself. Their names were Joe and Solly and they were identical twins. Both of them were excellent snooker players, but Solly was in fact a much better player than Joe. There is a story told about a game that Joe was playing in the Cosmo for a large bet with a player who was as good, if not better, than himself. They had played two games and the score was one each. In the final game Joe was not doing too well. Just then, Solly came in and a friend told him about Joe's situation. Solly went into the toilet and someone told Joe he should go there, which he did. Solly then came out to continue the game. In no time he cleared the balls on the table and won the game without the opponent being aware that he was dealing with a different player.

When I lived in Victoria Street, Dave Green and I would normally go to the Walworth Road *shul* on a Friday night, also on Saturday morning and the afternoon *mincha* service, and listen to a *drosha* (sermon) from Rabbi Matlin. It was the way of life at that time, and we had nothing better to do. Also, the choir in Greenville Hall had been disbanded when Cantor Rosenfield and Leo Bryll left Dublin.

There were many Jewish 'characters' around at that time. Joe Edelstein would have to be at the top of the list. It was said that he had been crossed in love and took to drink. He was a well-educated man and had written a number of books, including one about money-lenders which caused some controversy. When he was drunk he was never violent. He was well known to the police and the fire brigade. In the 1930s there were lamp posts at various corners painted red, and if a fire broke out in the vicinity someone would break a glass panel on the lamp post and press the alarm bell. The bell would summon assistance, and you had to stay at the spot to direct the fire brigade to the fire. If it was a false alarm you had to pay a £5 fine or go to prison. Joe Edelstein would set off the alarm and when the fire engines arrived they would find him there. He had no money to pay the fine. All he wanted was a warm cell in the police station. He was forever getting the fire brigade out on false alarms, and he always used the lamp post on the corner of Clanbrassil Street.

There was another character called Ruthstein. I think he stayed in the Iveagh Hostel in Bride Street. He always wore a fresh rose given to him by someone in the nearby flower market, and he always carried a walking stick. I also remember Gussie and Hymie Jackson, two brothers who I'm sure saw more days than meals. I never knew how they survived. They were rag and bone men. They were very polite and pleasant and I am glad to say that nobody took advantage of them. They were always available to make up a *minyan* (ten men needed to have a Jewish service). I'm sure they were helped by the Board of Guardians.

During the years from the mid-1920s to the end of 1940 the community buzzed with activity, and it was a great time for young Jewish boys and girls. It seemed that everyone was involved in various organisations and committees. The Jewish Debating Society was one of the strong groups, with speakers like Herman Good, Joe Baker, Victor and Larry Elyan, Leonard Abrahamson, Jack Weingreen, Elyah and Julius Isaacson, and so many others. When there was notice of a debate with a non-Jewish society, you would have to go to the venue very early or else you would have to stand. At that time, the debates took place in the upstairs rooms of the caretaker's house in Greenville Hall.

Some years later, the formation of the Junior Debating Society opened up many opportunities for the young members. Peter Leon was our first chairman. He was studying law and was serving his apprenticeship with Herman Good who was established in Dawson Street. I was secretary of the society. Inter-visits were organised, and one of the first of these that I remember was in Manchester in 1932. We were all put up in people's houses. I remember that I stayed with a family called Yaffe. They were very orthodox and I was pleased to find that because of my upbringing I fitted in well. We were in Manchester for a long weekend and many friendships were made.

A return visit to Dublin by Manchester took place in the following year. There were also inter-visits with debating societies in Belfast and Glasgow. It was only when I went to Manchester with the Debating Society that I heard the expression 'anti-Semitism' for the first time. I heard it from a speaker who had just returned from a visit to Germany and gave us a very chilling account of what was going on there.

Simon Sevitt was our chairman when we went to Glasgow for the first time. I think this was in 1933. We travelled by ship from the North Wall in Dublin. The ship also carried cattle. We were entertained in Glasgow by a very friendly group of people who did everything they could to make our trip memorable. I stayed with a family called Golumbok. The father was the owner and editor of a paper called (I think) *The Jewish Echo*. On our second visit to Glasgow, Berk Citron and I stayed with a family called Epstein. This second visit coincided with Christmas and New Year, and the celebrations were very exciting.

I was taken to watch Rangers and Glasgow Celtic play football on New Year's Day. A crowd of over 80,000 people watched the match. I remember that we were in the Rangers side of the ground, and I favoured Celtic. My friend said 'Don't you dare cheer for Celtic.' I had never been at a game where the crowd was separated. I saw a mass of yellow at the opposite end of the ground, and the people over there saw nothing but the blue of Rangers.

By the mid-1930s, most of my friends and contemporaries were medical students, which begs the question why didn't I study medicine also. I still wonder why my parents sent me to a Catholic secondary school, when there were other schools such as Wesley where so many Jewish boys and girls studied and did so well. I never got the answer to that question. And another question is: why did I not think of continuing with my studies? Was it the fact that there was a family business to go into?

Harold Isaacson and Simon Sevitt were two of my closest friends.

Both of them were brilliant students. Both won scholarships that enabled them to have free education in Wesley College, and then full scholarships to Trinity College to study medicine. But they also needed pocket money. Simon's father had a private clothing and tailoring shop in Harcourt Place, so he had an advantage over some other boys. Harold's father, who was the beadle in the Adelaide Road Synagogue, worked as a dental mechanic and was able to give Harold a certain amount of pocket money. Harold himself was also quite enterprising; he gave grinds to struggling medical students preparing for exams. Sometimes, if Simon was short of money for a holiday or whatever, he would pawn one of the gold medals he had won. But he always redeemed his medals later. Harold and I went on a number of holidays together. I still remember a week in Bundoran and a memorable stay in Llandudno in Wales in 1936.

I can remember one Christmas when the pubs were closed. The three of us went to a police station where as 'doctors' we had a bottle of Smithwicks Ale or a bottle of Guinness. Other than in a hotel, it was the only place where one could get an alcoholic drink on Christmas Day, and it was free. I remember an occasion when Harold invited me to the anatomy room in Trinity College to see the dead bodies. I think he thought I would be squeamish, but he was mistaken.

On Saturday night, after the Sabbath was out, a favourite place to go to was Barron's in Clanbrassil Street. They served chicken soup, *wurst*, sausages and chips, and we would finish off with lemon tea. To me, Simon and Harold, this was living. I really missed these two friends when they left for England at the outbreak of World War II. The three of us would also go to tennis club or cricket club dances. On one Saturday night we decided to go to a tennis club dance in Glasnevin on the north side of Dublin. Harold and Simon were in residence in their respective hospitals, Simon in Baggot Street and Harold in the Meath, so we arranged to meet for a drink in a pub off

Dame Street before going on to Glasnevin.

I was there first. The pub was quite full and as I waited to be served I heard a loud voice shouting 'I would love to kill a Jewman.' I could hardly believe my ears. The pub became very quiet. Just then a barman came to take my order and I said to him, also in a loud voice, 'There's a man over there shouting that he would like to kill a Jewman. Would you tell him there's a Jewman here.' The barman said 'Don't mind him.' Then I saw a bleary-eyed man looking up from the 'snug' (a small private area) and I called over to him 'I hear you would like to kill a Jewman.' 'I would,' he said. 'Well,' I said, 'I'm a Jewman. Would you like to start on me?' 'Oh no. I didn't mean you,' he replied. With that two people went over to where he was sitting and put him out of the pub and some others wanted to buy me a drink. I wonder what the atmosphere would have been like if I had pretended not to hear. To be honest, I didn't even think of being afraid. I think the date of this incident was early in 1936, when murmurings of anti-Semitism were coming from Germany.

I was involved in another unpleasant incident in 1939 when a team from the Carlisle Sports Club went to Liverpool for a tennis match against a Macabbi side. As we were leaving to get the boat back to Dublin, we passed a group of 'Blackshirts'. They were shouting anti-Jewish propaganda and I stopped to argue with one of them. If a policeman had not intervened, there could have been a fight. I was never afraid to stand up to anti-Jewish remarks and I was well used to street fights. Two policemen escorted our team to the boat and there was no further trouble, but we got a glimpse of what was going on in England.

Another friend of mine, Leslie Isaacson, had also decided to do medicine and was studying for the entrance exam. His father had a jewellery shop on the main street of Dún Laoghaire. In the early 1930s, a jeweller was allowed to practice as an optician. Leslie often helped out in the shop and had observed his father testing people's eyes and prescribing glasses for them. He persuaded me to let him test my sight. Having tested my eyes, he told me that my left eye was weaker than my right one. He said he would get me a pair of glasses if I would get him a pair of trousers. As Leslie took a rather small size, I was able to find a length of grey flannel material in the factory to make the trousers for him. So a deal was done: I got a pair of glasses and Leslie got a pair of trousers. His prescription proved to be correct, because many years later when I had my eyes tested it was found that there was indeed a weakness in my left eye.

When I was working in my father's factory, up to the time when I left to set up my own business in 1942, I was the official 'surgeon' in the factory. I was called whenever a girl got her finger caught in a machine or if the needle of the machine penetrated her finger. The first thing I did was to remove the needle from the machine. I would then examine the finger to see if the whole needle was in the finger; if it was I would pull the needle out of the finger with a pliers. In most cases the needle came out, but if it was broken I had to make sure that no part of it was left in the finger. Otherwise I would have to send her to Jervis Street hospital nearby. Fortunately that never happened.

One of my lasting memories as a youth was seeing Alfie Byrne TD, who was Lord Mayor of Dublin between the years 1930 and 1939. He was the longest serving Lord Mayor in the history of Lord Mayors. He was the most popular man in Dublin, and was to be seen nearly every day on the streets of Dublin, stopping and talking to people. He must have shaken more hands than all the Lord Mayors that came after him. He was often seen in Moore Street talking to the stallholders and hearing their grievances. He shook my hand many times when I happened to meet him, and he always made me feel important. He was a man of the people.

# 7  Sports Round-up

I was involved in sport of one kind or another from a very early age. When I met one of my schoolmates from St Catherine's recently, he said he has never forgotten an occasion when I was playing in a rugby match against the Boys' Brigade. I punched a fellow bigger than myself because he made an offensive remark about me. I still remember the game. It was played in the Boys' Brigade grounds in Dolphin's Barn. I could only have been eleven or twelve years old and even at that age I would not take insults from anyone.

When we were young we were very fond of football, and our favourite soccer team was Shamrock Rovers. For some reason it happened to be the team that most Jewish boys followed. We always went to see them play when the match was in Dublin, and we always cheered when they scored. They were the top club in the league and won the challenge cup more often than any other team. My older brother Hymie and younger brother Louis were devoted Rovers fans also. Along with Maurice Woolfson they would travel by bus to wherever Shamrock Rovers were playing in the country.

Hymie was normally a very quiet person, but the moment Rovers came onto the pitch he changed completely. He would shout, fling his arms everywhere, and only saw the green hoops on the Rovers shirts. Maurice and Louis were also staunch supporters, but Hymie was out on his own. Once, in Sligo, when Rovers were playing Sligo they were leading one goal to nil and Sligo were awarded a penalty. As the Sligo man was about to take the kick, Hymie jumped over the fence and kicked the ball away from the spot. It was Louis who told me about this, but when I asked if they were put out of the grounds he couldn't remember.

Many sporting events were held in the Phoenix Park, one of the largest public parks in Europe. Gaelic football, hurling, motorbike and motorcar racing were popular. Nathan Lepler, known to his colleagues as 'Lep', was a motorbike enthusiast. He started the Leinster Motor Cycle and Light Car Club, and he encouraged Jack Toohey to take up car racing.

Jack was always keen on motorcars and it was not long until the Ford Motor Company in Smithfield chose him to drive for them. I remember him driving a red car in a race in Phoenix Park. The track was the main road that circled the Park and I watched him overtaking other cars in some daring manoeuvres. It was no wonder that his father worried about his safety, but I don't think he was ever injured. The club started by Nathan Lepler is still going strong. Incidentally, Lep won many trophies on his motorbike. He also took part in the Monte Carlo Rally and finished the course.

Sometimes, we would watch the polo games that were played in Phoenix Park. It was very exciting to see the horses thundering around the enclosed area at full speed. There was cricket to watch also and the zoo to visit. And everything was free, except the zoo.

When I was about fifteen, a number of Jewish boys got together and formed a soccer club. We called ourselves New Vernon after a Jewish club that played in Dublin some years earlier. They had a very good record. One of their players had joined a well known club called Home Farm, and was chosen to play in the youths international games which he did with great distinction. This was Charlie Racusin. Charlie's brother Simon who had played for Vernon was asked to join a senior team called Dolphin. Dolphin's ground was in Harold's Cross.

I can name some of the team we started out with in New Vernon. There was myself, the two Orkin boys Simon and Jack, Manny Chaiken, Elliot Gutkin, Hymie and Stanley Robinson, Louis

Bookman and Max Bernstein. We had a very good team and the fact that we had Mendel Stein in goal saved us many times. We had to change in the open in Phoenix Park until we were allotted a changing room. The games were usually played in winter and when it rained we had to make sure that our clothes were properly covered. We played some great matches with various non-Jewish teams, and we were often applauded by people who stopped to watch the game. Some time later, we were allotted a room in the pavilion, which was a great bonus.

Carlisle Sports Club, which was founded in 1918 in Parkmore Drive, Terenure, enabled the young and not so young to take part in all kinds of sporting activities. Cricket was the main sport and Carlisle was a formidable team in the cricket league. They had some outstanding players, many of whom were chosen to play for Ireland. Among them were Louis Bookman, Sonny Hool and Louis Jacobson. Louis Bookman was an outstanding footballer also and played for an English club.

Cricket played a very important part in the sporting activities of the young people. Many schoolboys became prominent through playing for Ireland at school level and also at inter-provincial level. Some of the older club members took a tremendous interest in the team. Who will ever forget Lizzie Hool, Dick Weiner, George Hool, Willie Samuels, Louis Mushatt and so many others? There was great support for the club in the Jewish community, including from stalwarts like Jack Roberts and Alf Solomons. They made an important contribution to Carlisle's history. In later years, the Molin brothers played a prominent part in the Carlisle Cricket Club. Rodney was a regular member of the Irish team and his son Greg also played for Ireland. Another Jewish boy who played for Ireland was Rodney Bernstein.

There were five tennis courts in constant use in the early spring and up to the end of the summer. Tennis was the second of the major sports played in Carlisle, but the club didn't have great success in this area. However, a club member, Brian Ellis, who was studying at Trinity College, captained the Trinity team. Many dances were held in the small pavilion and they were always packed. Carlisle also had a few non-Jewish members. Des Hennessy and Frank Tate were two of them and they were very popular. And I still remember some of those who emigrated in the 1930s, including Cecil and Leslie Warnock, loyal members of the cricket team, and a friend of theirs, Ronnie Brass. They went to Australia when they qualified as doctors, and Leslie Copeman and Elyah Berstock went to England.

In 1930 a table tennis section was formed. I'm pretty sure that there are not too many people left who actually know how it came to be set up. I was one of the founder members, and I have a clear memory of what happened. It was started in the home of Ann and Charlie Gold when they lived on the Lower Kimmage Road. They put a table tennis top on their dining table, and it developed from there. Ann and Charlie were keen players and Ann played a very good game. Other players were Barney Noyek, Alf Solomons, Harold Isaacson, Dave Green, Harry Collins and myself. It was Harry Collins who raised the standard of the game. He was a big man but very agile and his flick along the right hand side was nearly always a winner.

As more people wanted to play, the venue was switched to the top of the caretaker's house at the back of Greenville Hall. After some time there, it moved to the big hall of Greenville Rooms. There were five tables and they were used three or four nights of every week. A team was formed with Harry Collins as No. 1. I can remember his games against Cyril Kemp, the Ireland No. 1. Carlisle always maintained a high place in their section of the league and provided several members of the Irish team. One of them was Harry Collins's brother Mick. Mick had come to Dublin to join Harry who by this time had established a large wholesale electrical company. Another who represented Ireland on a few occasions was Hubert Wine.

It is worth recalling that Chaim Herzog, later President of Israel, and his younger brother Jack were members of Carlisle. They were not sporting types, but I can remember playing tennis with Jack. They left Dublin in 1937 to go with their parents to Israel, where both of them rose to become important figures. Unfortunately, Jack died at the peak of his career when he was Ambassador to the United States. I am proud to be able to say that we were friends.

Many members of the community played rugby, but mostly they played for other clubs. As far as I know, the only Jew who played rugby for Ireland was Dr Bethel Solomons who later became Master of the Rotunda Hospital. Louis Jacobson played for Trinity. He was unlucky that Karl Mullen was around at the same time. Otherwise, I'm sure he would have played hooker for Ireland. If I were asked to name the most outstanding Jewish sportsman of my years in sport, I would have no hesitation in naming Louis Jacobson. He was wicket keeper for Ireland on many occasions and also excelled in golf.

My father's factory was located in Smithfield in a very large square. The Smithfield Motor Company was beside us and Irish Distillers was a little further up. Every week (on Thursday, I think) a market was held in the square. Horses and donkeys were bought and sold. I remember seeing young boys running alongside ponies, showing them off to potential buyers. Donkeys were also very much in demand. All in all it was a very colourful market and the trading went on all day.

One of the employees in the factory was a young man who was an excellent footballer. He was a junior international and a regular player on the Irish team. His name was Jimmy Long. He knew that I was a keen soccer player and asked me to me to join the team of the union in the factory. It was called the Workers' Union of Ireland and had headquarters in Fishamble Street, just off Christchurch Place. The union was run by Jim Larkin, who was often to be seen striding through the building.

I played for the team and did very well, scoring frequently. I played centre forward. After a year I was asked to play for Glenard. They were in a higher league. In my first game I scored three goals and a penalty. I thoroughly enjoyed playing for Glenard for a few years.

Then I made friends with the son of a shopkeeper in the area. His name was Tommy Hand, and he enticed me to join the Clontarf Rugby Club on the north side of the city. I was picked to play on the third A team, which was the club's fourth team. Except for one game in St Catherine's School, I had never played rugby before. But my knowledge of football seemed to impress some members of the committee, and I was picked to play on the second team for my next game. I made a lot of friends among the players and played with Clontarf for many years. During this time I was also invited to play with Dublin Rovers on Sundays. We would go by coach to provincial towns. One was Athlone, another Mullingar. Some members of the team were international rugby players and I was very pleased to be included in such company. I remember the games with Dublin Rovers as if they only happened today.

There was one unpleasant incident during the time I played for Clontarf. It happened after a home game. When we had showered and dressed, members of the team would have a few drinks at the bar in the club. I would always take my turn to buy a round of drinks, and it would be either the first or second round as my capacity would only be for two or three beers. We used to split up into groups of four or five. Once I had paid for a round, I could then drop out. On this particular day, a member of the team who had been drinking with another group of players came over to our group and started making nasty remarks to me. I was very taken aback because we always got on well together when we were playing a match. When I got my composure back I looked at him. He was a big burly fellow, a typical rugby forward. I said to him 'If you are trying to pick a fight with me you have picked the wrong person, because I am not the slightest bit afraid of you.' Members of the team intervened and we were separated before anything happened. Anyway, my status was raised because of the way I stood up to him.

The Jewish Boxing Club was started in 1935. The patrons were Victor Newman (chairman), Dr Norman Jackson, Robert Briscoe TD who was the only Jewish member of the Dáil, and Dr Harry Robinson who had retired as a ship's doctor. I joined the club in 1936, after watching a contest between the Jewish Boxing Club and another club. I happened to be sitting beside Bill Isaacson whose two nephews were also club members. We watched a few contests in which the Jewish boys were clearly outclassed, but they put up an excellent performance. Then there was another contest in which the Jewish boy was not good. I said to Bill that he should not have been allowed into the ring. He replied, 'It's easy for you to talk; could you do any better?' My answer was that if I couldn't do better I wouldn't box at all. I then decided to join the club. I had been involved in many street fights and I was well able to use my fists, but boxing in a ring is totally different from street fighting.

There were two trainers, Mick and Tommy Maloney, helping to train the boys. Mick took a great interest in me and showed me many ways of attacking an opponent and defending myself. When the club had its next inter-club contest I was paired with a soldier who appeared to be much heavier than me. However, his knowledge of boxing was poor and I managed to knock him out in the second round. I boxed at welterweight, which is 10st 7lbs. There were more inter-club contests that I won, and we had a new trainer named Mick Hayes who was also a former boxer. He persuaded me to enter a league competition for the South Dublin area. I had six contests in this league and I won all of them.

Then I had to box the winner of another area league, and I also won that. At this stage I was in the final of the County Dublin boxing championship, which I won after a really hard contest. But I was having problems at home trying to explain to my mother how I got a black eye. I told her I had got hit in the eye with a ball when I was playing tennis. I thought I had got away with it.

I must have impressed some clubs with my boxing, as I was invited by a club called Avona to train with their boys. At that time Avona was the leading club in Dublin. I took up the invitation and there is no doubt that I learned more skills training with some of their members. I certainly enjoyed my boxing years and I became friendly with many non-Jewish boys including Frankie Kerr, Ernie Smith and Gerard Coleman to name just a few. They and many others brought great credit to Ireland with their skills. Certainly they did not get the rewards that were to be won in other sports. Maybe this was because of their working-class background.

Simon Sevitt usually accompanied me for my fights. He would act as my 'second' and tell me how he thought I was doing. Because of his sight he never took up boxing himself. It is amazing that when you are involved in a boxing contest you don't feel your opponent's punches until you look at yourself in the mirror. I'm sure my father knew that I was boxing but never passed a remark, because nearly all the staff in the factory knew that I had won the County Dublin championship.

The training we were getting began to improve, and many of the boys won contests. Uckey Fine, Billy Cormick, Berk Citron, Sydney Curland and Maurice Weinsummer (who was a great favourite with the public) gave excellent performances and we all received very generous applause from the non-Jewish spectators. Freddy Rosenfield, who joined later, was also an excellent boxer and was a great credit to the club. I decided to quit boxing, mostly because of the opposition at home. But I was very annoyed when I saw a boy I had beaten in a previous contest winning the Irish welterweight championship.

About a year later, when I visited the doctor because I was having breathing problems, it was discovered that I had a broken nose and would need an operation. I didn't tell my parents anything about this. I spoke to Frank Tate, one of the few non-Jewish members of the Carlisle Sports Club. Frank was a doctor and was house surgeon in the Meath Hospital. He arranged for me to have the operation and said 'If anybody asks any questions about your work, just say you are a second year medical student.' Nobody asked any questions.

I remember the operation very clearly. The surgeon was a Mr Montgomery. I lay on a table and a nurse put a red rubber sheet over my body. I was given a local anaesthetic and I can still feel the rasp of the knife cutting along the bone in my nose. The operation did not take long. The nurse plugged my nose with cotton wool and I was put into a waiting room. After two hours the nurse replaced the cotton wool and then I walked home. I don't remember what explanation I gave my mother, but I stayed at home all that day and the next day. On the third day I returned to the hospital to have the dressing removed, and then went back to work immediately.

The Dublin Macabbi Golfing Society was founded in 1933 by a group of eleven people who met in a room over a shop at Kelly's Corner. The group included Eddie Barron, David Glick, Dr Lionel Shrago, Maurice (Mottle) Buchalter, Phil Buchalter, Sam (Schmerca) Jackson, Sidney Ellis, Willy Smullen, Jack Ellis and Kay Kernoff. I think Barney Leventhal was also a member of the group. They enjoyed playing golf, but being Jewish they found it very difficult to join non-Jewish clubs. But there were some exceptions. Monty Buchalter was a member of Castle Golf Club, and I'm sure there were a few more.

They were men of vision whose aims extended beyond the original Golfing Society. They knew that the young members of the community had little chance of being able to join any golf club, and they were looking into the possibility of setting up their own club.

When World War II broke out in September 1939, the Society decided that the time was ripe to look for a suitable area for a golf course. The Society began to grow when these plans became known and already there were fifty members. It was left to Harry Barron to clinch a deal to purchase a plot of land on which the golf club was built.

On 5 April 1944, a historic meeting was held in Zion Schools and Edmondstown Golf Club was established. It was reported that the land and buildings at Edmondstown had been acquired for the sum of £2,892 and consisted of over 75 acres. The report went on to inform the meeting that a well-known Scottish golf architect had designed the layout of nine holes, and on 21 April 1944 the first Captain, Harrie Barron, drove off the first tee to hearty applause.

There was tremendous support for the new club. Money began to flow in from people who wanted to play and also from the older members of the community. Now they had a club of their own and would no longer have to ask for permission to play on other golf courses. Many of the older members will never forget that it was due to religious prejudice that Edmondstown came about in the first place. The founders had the satisfaction of creating a club that would be open to all. It attracted a large number of non-Jewish golfers who were given five-day membership.

I joined Edmondstown Golf Club in 1948. I relied on Bernie Freeman and Victor Enoch, both of whom had cars, to pick me up at the bridge on Orwell Road. Many of the members who had cars would normally pass this way on their way to Edmondstown, so I never worried about getting there. Later that year I had my own transport, but I still took a lift with either Bernie or Victor.

The club has come a long way since its foundation in 1944. What started as a nine-hole course has become an eighteen-hole course. The clubhouse has had major alterations over the years. Today the club is professionally managed, it is financially sound, and it has many new and younger members who are only too willing to give their time to the various committees responsible for club activities. As it enters its second half-century, Edmondstown Golf Club recalls those eleven founding members whose vision ensured for their children and grandchildren the right and freedom to play golf without hindrance or permission from anyone.

*14 Greenville Terrace, where I was born in May 1915, and lived with my parents and seven brothers and sisters.*

*My father and mother.*

*Members of the Adelaide Road Synagogue in the later 1920s, with members of the Jewish Boy Scout and Girl Guide troops in attendance: Front row, left to right: Rev. Gudansky, Chief Rabbi Dr Herzog, Arthur Newman, an unknown visitor, W. Nurock. Back row, left to right: Mr Cormick, Edwin Solomons, David Cowan, Bernard Shillman, J. M. Elliman.*

*The interior of Adelaide Road Synagogue, which opened in 1892 and closed in 1999.*

*Interior of Greenville Hall Synagogue, opened in 1925.*

*Some of the choir in the Greenville Hall Synagogue in the 1930s. In the front is Rev. Cantor Rosenblatt, I am behind the candlestick on his right. Also in the picture (from left) Izzy Rosen, Teddy Lewis, and at the back Dave Green, Joe Cristol and Sam Jacobs.*

*Rabbi E. E. Gavron (1866–1941), my Hebrew teacher, and the rabbi at the Lombard Street* shul, *was a great influence on me and many others in the Jewish community. (Irish Jewish Museum)*

*Rabbi Matlin of Walworth Road Synagogue.*

*Ettie Steinberg from Dublin and her young son Leon were the only Irish citizens to die in the Holocaust. Here she is, pictured at her wedding in 1937 at the Greenville Hall Synagogue.*

*Riv and I were married in the Greenville Hall Synagogue on 9 August 1942.*

*The Dublin Jewish Boxing Club 1937/8. Front row, left to right: W. Briscoe, F. Isaacson, V. Newman (Chairman), M. Hayes (Trainer), J. Briscoe, R. Briscoe TD. Middle row, left to right: J. Resnik, H. Woolfe LDSI, M. Cohen, N. Harris, S. Isaacson, B. Citron, T. Glasser, D. M. Robinson LDSI, Dr L. H. Robinson. Back row, left to right: Dr N. Jackson, I. Green, P. Levine, J. Woolfe, S. Levene, I. Sevitt.*

*On holiday in Galway in 1936.*

*Valerie, Riv and myself on holiday in the USA*

*Riv and myself in 1943.*

*April 1944: Harrie Barron, the first Captain of Edmondstown Golf Club drives himself into office. From left: P. Levine, 'Snob' Jackson, M. D. Buchalter, H. 'Jumbo' Woolfe, M. 'Monty' Buchalter, Bessie Woolfe, David Glick, Sol White, Henry Barron, Jack Toohey, Dr Joe Lewis, B. Leventhal, L. Lapedus, E. Barron.*

*Clanbrassil Street in the 1960s—only a few of the Jewish shops remain, such as Erlich on the right and Rubenstein on the left.*

*Rabbi M. Brown, a very saintly man. (Irish Jewish Museum)*

*Beila Erlich in her shop in Clanbrassil Street. (Irish Jewish Museum)*
*Originally just a butcher, she stocked more and more kosher products as*
*other shops went out of business.*

*Our daughter Valerie graduated aged 54
with a degree in psychotherapy and
counselling.*

*Riv and myself, with our two granddaughters Dalia and Tasha.*

# 8 Synagogues and Rabbis

There were numerous synagogues in Dublin when I was growing up. The three main *shuls* were Adelaide Road, Greenville Hall and the Temple in Lombard Street. A number of smaller synagogues also flourished. Adelaide Road *shul* was built in 1892 at a cost of £5,000, and extended in 1925. It continued to serve the community until it was closed in 1999, over a hundred years later. When I was a child, Rev. Gudansky (father of Herman Good) was the minister, Rev. Roith was the reader and Joe Isaacson was the beadle. Rev. Roith was also a *mohel* (circumsiser), and a busy *mohel* at the time.

When Rev. Gudansky retired in 1938, the synagogue appointed Rabbi Theodore Lewis to succeed him. Rabbi Lewis had just returned from Europe, having qualified as a Rabbi. In fact there were fears for his safety as the news of anti-Semitic attacks continued to reach Dublin, and it was a relief when it became known that he was safe. He was the only practising Irish Rabbi at that time, and he served the community well for a short period until he accepted a call from a synagogue in Rhode Island, USA.

In 1939, the synagogue in Adelaide Road got the services of a new Cantor named Nandor Freilich, and a choirmaster named Philip Model. Two years later, Nandor married Eudice Buchalter, a first cousin of my wife Riv, and they had two children, Eleanor and Jonathan. Nandor was very popular. He enjoyed sports and loved to play billiards in the Literary Club, but in the choir and in the synagogue he was very strict. When he died in 1949 at a comparatively young age, he was greatly missed by many in the community.

After a number of years as a widow, Eudice met Geoffrey Fabian.

Geoff and his sister Gerda had been evacuated from Germany before the war. They were sent first to England, then to Canada, and eventually returned to England when the war was over. Gerda went to live in Leeds, and Geoff eventually came to Dublin where he got a position with Jack Tuohy. Eudice and Geoff met at a bridge tournament around 1955, and before long they decided to get married.

Geoff left his job at Tuohy's and joined Eudice who had a picture framing business on Aston Quay, near O'Connell Street. The business, which traded as Charles Webb, had been established many years previously by Eli Buchalter. Even though Geoff knew nothing about picture framing when he met Eudice, he learned quickly. Within a very short time he transformed the business and they opened another shop in the Grafton Arcade, off Grafton Street.

Most of Geoff's family had been killed in the Holocaust. He used to go to Leeds to see his sister there, and he had an elderly aunt living in Switzerland whom he visited every year. He wasn't aware of any other relatives. Geoff had very little knowledge of Judaism when he married Eudice. She came from a very religious background. He respected her for her beliefs; I was given the honour of conducting the *Pesach* service for a number of years.

Then he began to take an interest in reading Hebrew (the language of the prayer book and the Scriptures) and learning to read *Ivrith* (Hebrew as spoken in Israel today). He used every moment of spare time in the shop to read the *Siddur* (prayer book) in Hebrew and within a comparatively short time he was able to conduct the Passover service himself. He also learned to read newspapers and write letters in *Ivrith*.

He decided to go to live in Israel and managed to convince Eudice, who was reluctant at first to leave Dublin and family. But her two children, Eleanor and Jonathan Freilich, were grown up and living in London. So they put their house on the market and it sold very quickly. They also sold the shop and when this was done they were ready to leave. By then, Geoff had discovered that he had a cousin living in Israel. This was very important, as it meant that he already had family there. They soon found an apartment in Natanya and settled happily into a new way of life.

When Nandor Freilich and Philip Model organised a choir for Adelaide Road, they called on some of those who had been in the Greenville Hall choir. Philip asked me to join, but I was in business on my own and couldn't commit myself to the choir at that time. I eventually joined in the late 1950s, and I was welcomed by Morry Gordon whom I knew very well through business. I enjoyed singing in the Adelaide Road Synagogue which, to me, had the appearance of a cathedral. Herman Good was President, and I admired the way he was able to keep the decorum. One look from him was sufficient to stop you talking and then he would smile as if to say 'Thank you' when you stopped. He and Sam Crivon, who was also in the box along with Morry Gordon and Eli Schwartzman, lent dignity to the service.

For some years before the Adelaide Road Synagogue was closed, the number of people attending services had been declining. The *shul* was kept going by loyal members, but those whose children and grandchildren had joined the Terenure Synagogue gradually moved there to be with them. It became apparent that a decision would have to be made as to whether the two *shuls* should be amalgamated. The difficult decision was made and the synagogue which had celebrated its centenary in 1992 closed its doors on 31 May 1999.

The closing of the synagogue was very painful for people who thought it could never happen in their time. There were many meetings before it was finally agreed to amalgamate with Terenure, where there was adequate room to accommodate any members of the Adelaide Road Synagogue who wished to go there. The decision was taken on the understanding that when the building in Adelaide Road was sold the money would be used to build another synagogue behind the existing one in Terenure. The new synagogue would accommodate Adelaide members and Terenure members, and would also be a meeting place.

At the Deconsecration Ceremony of the Adelaide Road Synagogue the President, Martin Simmons, opened the proceedings and gave a brief talk about the reasons for closing the *shul*. He then called on the Life President, Hubert Wine, to address the large gathering of members. Hubert thanked various colleagues for their support during his time as President. He mentioned in particular Martin Simmons, Seton Menton and Don Buchalter who helped him to keep the *shul* open. He praised Cantor Shulman for his devotion to the *shul* and he thanked the ladies' committee for their outstanding work.

Hubert said that he was on the Council of this synagogue for fifty years and the day of its deconsecration was one of the saddest days in his life.

Speaking about the history of the *shul* that was built in 1892, he recalled many of the members including his own father and grandfather who contributed their time and their efforts for the *shul* that was now about to close. The late Morrie Gordon was among those whose special contribution was remembered; he used to organise the *Chanuka* parade of Boy Scouts and Girl Guides every year.

Referring to some important events in the history of the Adelaide *shul*, Hubert recalled the visit of Cearbhall O'Dalaigh in December 1974, when a special service was held to mark his inauguration as President of Ireland. In 1985, when Chaim Herzog made a State visit to Ireland as President of Israel he came to the *shul* for a special service in his honour. It was here that he had read his *Bar Mitzvah* portion as a boy. Hubert went on to speak about the Jewish contribution to Ireland at many different levels. Recalling that twenty-three Jewish sportsmen had played for Ireland, he was happy to be the first President of the congregation to be invited to participate in the Annual Ecumenical Service held in 1987 in thanksgiving for the gift of sport.

He reminded his audience that Adelaide Road had been the home of the Ireland-Israel Friendship League for many years. He paid tribute to Brian Quinn for his efforts to promote goodwill between Ireland and Israel through his work with the League. Concluding his address, he said: 'This is not the end of the Dublin Hebrew Congregation. I would like you to think that this great congregation, now in its 108th year and moving to a new site, will proudly continue for many years as the Dublin Hebrew Congregation and along with the Terenure congregation will continue serving the community as it always has done.'

Using texts from the *Torah* and *Qoheleth*, Chief Rabbi Gavin Broder reflected on the significance of moving the Ark and the bringing together of two *shuls*. He knew that there were people present who had sat in the same seats for seventy years, and some of them had inherited the seats from their fathers and grandfathers. He repeated that there is no substitute for personal involvement. He called on the congregants to take on the move from Adelaide Road not just collectively but also individually. He praised the members of the community for their service and dedication, and wished them every success for the future.

Chief Rabbi Broder was followed by Rabbi Mirvis who delivered an outstanding address. Rabbi Mirvis arrived in Dublin with his wife and young children in 1982 and stayed for ten wonderful years. He recalled precious and moving moments during the *Rosh Hashanah* and *Yom Kippur* services in Adelaide Road and said that the closing of the *shul* made him very sad. But he said it was the right thing to do and a brave decision to make. 'In Jewish history, synagogue buildings have never been an end in themselves … In Jewish tradition there are no blessings for buildings, only for the people in the buildings … The finest memorial to the Adelaide Road Synagogue will be the passing on of Jewish tradition from one generation to the next.'

He spoke in glowing terms of what the Adelaide *shul* and members meant for him and his family. When they heard that the synagogue was to close, his children begged him to take them back to Dublin to have one last look at the *shul* where they had spent ten happy years. The whole family came back for one day to see that magnificent building again. During his ten years in Dublin, the members had come to love and admire Ephraim Mirvis and his wife Valerie, and his presence and his words on this very significant occasion were deeply appreciated.

Following these speeches, *Sefer Torahs* (sacred scrolls) were removed from the Ark. Nine members of the Council each carried a *Sefer Torah* around the *shul* three times, before they were transferred to the *Minyan* Room. From there they would be brought to Terenure, where they would be welcomed on the following evening. Cantor Shulman, who had conducted the entire service along with the choir of young boys, concluded with a prayer. Martin Simmons, the President, delivered the closing address of the Deconsecration Ceremony which marked the end of an era of more than one hundred years. Many members held back tears as they remembered the glory days of the Adelaide Road Synagogue. The building was sold later for over £6 million. This money will go a long way towards the cost of building the planned new synagogue in Terenure.

The Greenville Hall Synagogue was behind the new *shul* that opened for service in 1925. Rev. Jaffe was the reader then. I remember him as a very dignified person with a white beard. Mr Papkin was the beadle. He was a very kind man. He was married but did not have any children. He and his wife were good friends of my parents and often visited us in Greenville Terrace. From what I can remember, there was a certain amount of rivalry between the two synagogues. The Adelaide Road synagogue was always referred to as the *Englishe shul* by Greenville Hall members. It may be that the latter thought they were more orthodox than the former. Anyway, that rivalry persisted. The original synagogue at the rear of the new *shul* was turned into a reception hall where most of the marriages were celebrated. It was also used for dances, and people will have fond memories of events that took place there.

In the years before the Greenville Hall Synagogue closed because of diminishing numbers, Rev. Gittleson was the reader. He was referred to by some of the members as 'the head cook and bottle washer'. He was born in Dublin, and I have always felt that he was not given enough credit for his contribution to the community. He loved taking the service in *shul*, he was a *shochet* in the abattoir, he was a *mohel* (performing circumcision on boys), and took on many other duties. The community was his life and he never wanted payment for the extra services he carried out. When he became ill his wife begged him to see a doctor, but to no avail. He was either afraid to go to the doctor or afraid of what the doctor might find wrong with him. He died suddenly, and was found to have had diabetes.

The attendance at Greenville Hall was much smaller after the opening of the synagogue in Terenure in 1953, but Rev. Gittleson was determined to keep the *shul* going as long as there was a *minyan* of ten men. I continued to attend with my father, who was a life-long member. Often, I would look around the near empty *shul* and recall some of the stalwarts of the community: Philip Baigel, Mr Price, Reuben Segal, Mick Jacobson, Jacob Zlotover, Mr Isaacson, Louis Freedman, Isaac Tomkin, Morris Ellis, Mr Robinson and his sons Abe and Henry who would always come to the Greenville *shul* from their home in Carlow for *Yom Tov* (celebration).

I remember that the Muslims who were coming to Ireland at that time offered to buy the Greenville Hall Synagogue. The figure mentioned was around a quarter of a million pounds, but Rev.

Gittleson would not hear of it. They wanted to convert the synagogue to a mosque. When Rev. Gittleson died suddenly a year or so later, the synagogue was sold for much less than the Muslims had offered. The remaining members were never told how much the building was sold for, nor was there any meeting called to inform them of details regarding the sale. Personally, I regret that there was no Deconsecration Ceremony in the Greenville Hall Synagogue.

This was the end of a beautiful synagogue where I had attended regularly, celebrated my *Bar Mitzvah* and married. It is now used as a business centre. The Hebrew letters that were on the front of the building are no longer there. It is the same imposing building that it always was, but there is no indication that it was a synagogue. I hope something can be done about this, so that visitors to the Museum who see a photograph of the synagogue could then go to see it in reality.

The third *shul* was the Temple in Lombard Street. I do not know much about this particular *shul*, except that it catered for the many Jewish people living in the area. Rabbi Gavron, who was my *cheder* teacher, was the resident Rabbi of the Temple *shul*. When it closed in 1968, many of the members joined the Greenville *shul*. Rabbi Brown was one of the people who attended services in the Temple. He lived alone in Bloomfield Avenue when I was young. He was a small man, of slim build. He had a straggly beard and always wore a frock coat, winter and summer. I don't know where he came from. To me he seemed to be ageless and he always carried an umbrella. He was always around Clanbrassil Street. He attended morning and evening service in the Temple, and would be present whenever there was a *shiur* (religious discussion).

Issy Bernstein, who lived in Rosedale Terrace, just off Clanbrassil Street, told me that Rabbi Brown was a constant visitor to their home, and he, Issy, would go around the area once a month and collect a shilling from each of the *shul* members to give the money to the Rabbi who had no other means of support.

Recently, Max Bernstein told me another story about Rabbi Brown. One day he came visiting their home. He seemed to be agitated for some reason, and Max was told by his father to take the Rabbi home. When they got to the house the Rabbi collapsed. Max went next door, where the Caplins lived, to get help. Next, he ran to get a doctor who gave Rabbi Brown an injection to calm him down. Then they got the Rabbi into his own house and put him to bed. When the Rabbi appeared to be sleeping, Max went home and told his father what had happened. Some hours later they were astounded to hear tapping on the path outside their house, and knew that it could only be Rabbi Brown. The Rabbi was invited in and then he explained why he had come back. He wanted to know if he had said anything that could have offended anyone while he was being attended to.

One of the smaller synagogues was in Walworth Road. A number of Rabbis found themselves in Dublin for some reason, and it was felt that they deserved to be given their own place of worship. Rabbi Matlin was one of these, so Maurice Elliman, Mr Glick and Mr Watchman decided to buy two houses in Walworth Road and have a synagogue built conforming to every aspect of Jewish law. There were two floors in the joined houses. The ground floor was used for meetings and some festive occasions, with fitted kitchens. The *shul* was upstairs with the *bema* in the centre and Rabbi Matlin sat beside the Ark where the scrolls were kept. The women were at the back of the *shul*, right across the two joined houses, with net curtains shielding them from the men. I often saw the curtain being lifted by a woman to get a better look at some man. The *shul* held about 160 people and was always well attended.

The Friday night and *Shabbos* services were usually conducted by Mr Elliman and Mr Watchman. I can well remember Mr Elliman *davening* (praying). He had a very pleasant voice. Mr Watchman also took part in the service and he was the one who *layned* (read from the *Torah*). The *shul* was completed during 1918, but it had to close around 1975, due to decreasing numbers. This synagogue played a big part in the life of the Dublin community, at a time when almost the entire Jewish community lived within a half-mile radius of Walworth Road. I am delighted that the building is now being used as a museum.

The Irish Jewish Museum was the inspiration of Asher Benson. Asher came to Ireland in 1946, after serving with the British Army in India and Burma. Shortly after he arrived in Dublin he met Ida Silverman whose parents had been living in Drogheda, Co. Louth. Asher and Ida married and had two sons, who are now married and living in Dublin. Having become very interested in the history of the Jewish community in Dublin, Asher set up an exhibition in the Adelaide Road Synagogue of artefacts and pictures that he managed to procure from various members of the community. The exhibition took place in 1978. It was opened by Herman Good and was attended by Rabbi Cohen who was the Chief Rabbi of Ireland at that time. But the idea of a permanent museum to show the history of the community was always in Asher's mind, and a committee of interested people was formed to bring the project forward.

The Walworth Road building seemed perfect for housing the museum, but when this was proposed by the committee there was a storm of protest. Well-meaning people said the building should be sold and the money raised would be of more benefit to the community. But the committee went ahead with their plan. It was found that the building would need complete refurbishment, including a new roof. An appeal for funds was launched. An approach was also made to Ruairi Quinn, then Minister for Labour. He was interested in the project and promised that he would provide the labour, which he did. Money collected through fund-raising paid for materials, the work started and the whole building was refurbished in 1984.

I remember that there were small synagogues in Lennox Street and St Kevin's Parade. In St Kevin's Parade a small house was converted by a very orthodox group of people who no doubt thought that the other synagogues were not *frum* (orthodox) enough for them. Mr A. Steinberg and family, and Mr Wertzberger were leading members of this group. Mr Wertzberger had come to Dublin at the end of the 1920s and he was a friend of my parents. He had a small shop in his house in Clanbrassil Street. Coming up to the war and in the early years of World War II, he stocked a very large range of goods, including rationed items such as tea and sugar. Much of his stock was kept under the counter and sold to favoured customers. He had whiskey, brandy, cigarettes, *kosher* wine, and books in Yiddish by well-known authors. He also stocked Yiddish newspapers published in America.

Before Rabbi Herzog went to Palestine in 1937, Mr Wertzberger enlisted his help to raise money from members of the community to get his wife out of Czechoslovakia. The necessary funds were collected, but instead of bringing his wife out he used the money to pay her off. She gave him a *get* (divorce) and he brought a new wife back to Dublin. He came under a lot of criticism in the community, my mother didn't speak to him for some time and he lost many of his friends. But after a number of years people accepted his wife, who I must say was a very pleasant woman. He also managed to get his daughter out of Czechoslovakia, but where she went to I do not know.

There was also a synagogue on Lower Ormond Quay. It was a very quaint *shul* that had been converted from rooms in a house owned by a Mr Cohen. It had all the requirements for a *shul*. There was a small *bema* and an Ark that had two or more *Sefer Torahs* (scrolls containing the five books of Moses). It occupied two rooms on the ground floor, with a small section curtained off for the women.

The Ark was a work of art, all white, with pillars decorated to look like marble. The *shul* was used mainly by people who had a business in the area. There were many who had *Yahrzeit* (anniversary prayers) there for parents who had died. They would contact Mr Cohen who would be delighted to open the *shul* for the occasion.

There were three Cohen brothers, Louis, Isadore and Maurice, and if someone needed to say prayers they would phone a few regulars who would go to make up the *minyan* of ten men needed for the service. When I had a business in Dame Street, I would go at once whenever I was called. During the winter months I often attended the *shul* in Ormond Quay. I remember the Sabbath service being taken by Sydney Davis, who had a shop in Capel Street supplying office equipment. He had a very pleasant voice. When the Jewish Home of Ireland was established in 1950, the Ark from Mr Cohen's house was taken apart and placed in the synagogue of the Jewish Home.

Louis Cohen had an antiques shop in Liffey Street, near the river, and he also dealt in paintings. He was always willing to give advice to anyone who came to him. When the Jewish Home opened, he devoted much of his time to looking after the *shul*. He was to be seen there nearly every day, and it was taken for granted that when he died the Home would benefit from his estate. But this was not to be. On a visit to Israel he was so impressed by what he saw that he left the bulk of his estate to the Lubavitch movement.

His brother, Isadore Cohen, had an antiques shop in Upper Liffey Street and was usually to be found sitting on a chair outside the shop. If a customer showed an interest in an article, he would say that it was already sold. On one occasion I asked the price of something in the window. When he saw me he asked 'What do you want?' and before I could answer he shouted, 'I haven't got it.' He was a strange character.

Maurice was the youngest of the three Cohen brothers. He had a printing works in part of the house on the Quays. I did a fair amount of business with him and found him most agreeable. When Edmondstown Golf Club opened in 1944 he was one of the first members. But he never played golf on *Shabbos* or on any of the festivals.

The Cohen brothers had a sister who married Robert Isaacson, a brother of Julius and Max Isaacson. I remember that Robert Isaacson, Louis Baker (a brother of Manny Baker) and Michael Goldberg worked for my father as machinists when he had the factory on Ormond Quay. In those days it was not uncommon to have men working on sewing machines.

Larry Elyan and Moe Spain were the prime movers in the establishment of the Progressive Synagogue in 1946. Other supporters included Victor Enoch, George Morris, David Finkle, Hans Borchardt, Henry Lowe and Charlie Gold. There was always a strong orthodox community in Dublin, and there was division in the community when the plans of the progressive movement became known. I remember a meeting that took place in Zion Schools. Rabbi Herzog had come to speak against the project. However, despite all the opposition the Progressive Synagogue was opened and the membership has continued to increase over the years.

Rabbi Kokotek came from London for the opening service. Rabbi Brash was installed as minister and Dr Bethel Solomons was invited to be the first President. He was an excellent choice for the position of President, as he had a deep interest in the Jewish faith.

Men and women began to join and regular services were held each Friday night and Saturday morning—the main service being on Friday. Moe Spain organised a choir of men and women, including Joe Cristol who had many years' experience of singing in choirs. The mixed choir was excellent and I can remember listening to them with great pleasure. Hebrew classes were also started. I used to collect Victor Enoch's two boys, Michael and Stephen, and also Susan

Angel and Jeremy Borchhardt every Sunday to take them with our children to their class. Some years later, Jeremy became President of the synagogue.

The Progressive Synagogue continues to attract people, and it accepts members from the many mixed marriages. My own opinion is that it is doing something worthwhile when it attracts these people along with their children to the services in Leicester Avenue. Otherwise they could be lost to the community. I have attended a few of the services there and I have appreciated the decorum and the singing of the choir. But it is not for me with my upbringing, and I am too long in the tooth to change.

From the 1930s onwards, members of the community began moving over the canal bridge and away from the Jewish quarter where I grew up. As families moved to Rathmines and later to Terenure, a group of men came together and decided to build a synagogue to cater for their needs. The group included Wolfe Freedman, Sam Noyek, Nat Mendel, Solly Marcus, Sam Fine, Erwin Goldwater, Harry Elliot and many others. The Rathmines Hebrew Congregation had been established in the mid-1930s and there was a synagogue on Grosvenor Road. When many of the young families moved to Terenure, a site was purchased there and fund-raising began for the building of the Terenure Synagogue which opened in 1953.

Sam Noyek was very involved in all aspects of the undertaking. He was very enthusiastic and gave his full support to the plans to provide a synagogue for the ever-increasing numbers of Jewish people living in the area. He was also in a position to supply at little cost the timber needed for the seating etc. and in this way to keep the expenses down. Sam attended the Terenure Synagogue regularly for morning and evening prayers. He was elected honorary Life President and thereafter devoted his entire life to the good of the *shul*. He was very practical, and I remember that when there were *Yahrzeit* prayers (for deceased relatives) he would have the box for charity donations under your nose, and he never had refusals. Few people are aware of the extent of Sam's generosity. But I know that it went beyond the needs of the Terenure *shul* and the Jewish community. When he was walking along the South Circular Road one day in the early 1940s, he saw young children running around barefoot. He went to the nearest convent and gave the nuns a cheque for £500—no mean sum of money at the time—to buy shoes for children in need of shoes

Sam Noyek continued to play an active part in the synagogue and in community affairs until he became ill. He died in the Adelaide Hospital on 9 June 1992. His coffin was brought to Terenure *shul* to honour him for his years of devoted service. In a packed synagogue, Rabbi Ephraim Mirvis spoke in glowing terms of his commitment to the Jewish community of Dublin. At his request his daughter Thelma, accompanied by Martin and children Wendy and Robin, brought his remains to be interred on the Mount of Olives in Jerusalem.

The Terenure *shul* had its own ministers from the beginning. Rev. Solly Bernstein, who was born in Dublin, is one who comes to mind. He conducted the Friday night and *Shabbos* services, and took upon himself the reading of the *Sedra* (portion of the law in the five books of Moses). He was a dedicated man who loved what he was doing. He also gave private lessons to boys preparing for *Bar Mitzvah*. He gave a lifetime of service to the Terenure *shul*.

The new synagogue began to attract more and more people. It was not that they preferred the Terenure *shul* to their own, but they found it more convenient since they were now living nearby, and many members of the community did not want to use transport to go to Greenville Hall or Adelaide Road for *Shabbos* and the festivals. And there was another reason also: members of other synagogues who had grandchildren living in the Terenure area wanted to be with them.

The ladies' committee formed in Terenure made an important contribution, and women like Ethel Freeman, Mrs Bunny Davis, Sally Green, Elsie Stein, Gittle Marcus and many more, helped to make the running of the synagogue a success. Strangely, only one member of the Jewish community decided to open a grocery shop in Terenure. This was Hilda Fine whose parents had a shop in Clanbrassil Street. Hilda knew what people needed with regard to Jewish food. She catered for their requirements and built up a thriving business.

Even though so many Jewish people moved to Terenure, no other shops were opened. There was a delicatessen that served soup, sausages, *wurst* and chips. This was owned by a son of the butcher, Abe Samuels. He did a steady business with young people coming from the Carlisle Sports Club, but had to close the shop after a few years owing to ill health. Clanbrassil Street continued to lure people who needed to be in a Jewish atmosphere and to get the gossip that you can only get in Jewish shops.

In February 1966 there was a serious fire in the Terenure Synagogue. This was an anti-Semitic attack carried out by one person. He gained entrance to the building and set fire to the area where the scrolls were kept. The caretaker raised the alarm. He phoned Nat Mendel, the President of the synagogue, and alerted the fire brigade. When Nat Mendel went into the *shul* the whole Ark was on fire and there was a man lying across one of the seats. He was groaning and appeared to be semi-conscious. The fire brigade came very quickly and the fire was brought under control within two hours. Three of the valuable scrolls were destroyed. Two others were saved but damaged, and it took two years to repair them. The man was taken to hospital and later charged, but found to be deranged. No other person was involved in this incident which was widely condemned. The total damage to the synagogue was estimated at £30,000.

When Rabbi Isaac Herzog left Dublin for Palestine in 1937, we had nobody to replace him as Chief Rabbi until Rabbi Immanuel Jakobovitz arrived in 1949. In the meantime, we had Dayan (Rabbi) Zalman Alony. Dayan Alony's wife was Rabbi Matlin's daughter. He was a kind and gracious person but his command of English was poor. He looked after the *kashrut* for the community and was very knowledgeable on the Jewish Law. After many years serving the Dublin community, Dayan Alony went to London to take up a position in the Beth Din there. The Beth Din is the highest authority for Jewish law in the UK and Ireland.

Rabbi Emmanuel Jakobovitz arrived in 1949. He was a Rabbi in London before he received a call to be the Chief Rabbi in Dublin. He and his wife moved into a house on Bloomfield Avenue off the South Circular Road. Both of them were very well liked. Rabbi Jakobovitz served the Dublin Jewish community with distinction and continued as Chief Rabbi until 1958 when he left to take up a position in New York. Later, he became Chief Rabbi of Great Britain, Northern Ireland and the British Commonwealth.

Chief Rabbi Jakobovitz was followed by Rabbi Isaac Cohen. He was a Rabbi in Edinburgh when he was called to take up the vacant position of Chief Rabbi in Dublin. He and his wife arrived in 1959. He took his position very seriously, and did not spare feelings when he addressed the members of the synagogue. When he addressed the people of Ireland on Passover and the New Year he was applauded by many non-Jews for his lucid explanation of the Festivals, and he was the first Rabbi to use the medium of television to bring better understanding between Jews and non-Jews. He was very respected outside the community.

When Rabbi David Rosen succeeded Rabbi Cohen as Chief Rabbi in 1979, he also used television to speak to the Irish people, and his successors have done likewise. Rabbi Rosen brought great dignity to the office of Chief Rabbi and he and his wife and children were very popular in the community. He was an eloquent speaker and people looked forward to his sermons. It was clear that he is a man whose main aim in life is justice for all human beings. He also spoke about individual rights and about how people should conduct themselves in relation to others. An important part of the role of the Rabbi is mediating in disputes that arise in the community. I can think for instance of one occasion when a Rabbi mediated in a breach of promise case, to prevent it going to law, and another when the Rabbi helped to smooth over an argument relating to business dealings. David Rosen and his family left Dublin in 1984 to live in Israel, where he continues his work to promote tolerance and understanding. He played an important part in the work that led to the establishment of diplomatic relations between Israel and the Vatican.

Rabbi Rosen set a high standard to be followed by his successor. Rabbi Ephraim Mirvis had come to Dublin in 1982 as minister to the Adelaide Road and Terenure Synagogues, while David Rosen was still Chief Rabbi of Ireland. When Rabbi Rosen left in 1984, he succeeded him immediately as Chief Rabbi. He undertook many roles beyond the office of Chief Rabbi and was always available to the community. His broadcasts helped in no small way to improve our relationships with our neighbours. He even found time for sport and could be seen wielding a cricket bat on the pitch at the Macabbi sports grounds. His wife Valerie gave him great support in his work and both of them left an indelible mark on our community.

In 1992, when he received a call from the Marble Arch synagogue in London, he had to accept it as he no doubt felt that he had to move on. Then he got a call to be the minister of the prestigious Finchley Road Synagogue, where a vacancy had occurred on the death of (Dublin-born) Rabbi Isaac Bernstein. He was sad to leave Marble Arch where he and his family were very happy. When I was on a visit to London I went to see him and he greeted me very warmly.

Rabbi Mirvis still has contact with some members of the

community in Dublin, and he and Valerie were invited to come over for the Deconsecration Ceremony in the Adelaide Road Synagogue in May 1999. On that occasion he addressed the congregation, recalling with fondness their association with the Dublin community and expressing great sadness at the closure of such a wonderful synagogue and the end of an epoch.

History was made in Dublin when Chief Rabbi Broder found himself seated with the other religious leaders in St Paul's Church, Mount Argus, on 22 November 1999. The occasion was the funeral of Jack Lynch, former Taoiseach (Prime Minister). The Chief Rabbi was accompanied by Estelle Menton, Chairperson of the Jewish Representative Council. Estelle has told members of the Terenure congregation that when they arrived at the church, she suggested that the Rabbi stay on the steps and she would sign the book of condolence for both of them. As she was signing the book she realised that Rabbi Broder was standing behind her. They were approached by an official who welcomed them, said there were seats reserved for them, and went forward with them to their places. It was an historic occasion, and an experience that will be remembered by the Rabbi for a long time.

In late 2001, Dr Yaakov Pearlman was appointed Chief Rabbi for the Dublin Community. Originally from Manchester, he came to Dublin from New York where had been working as a Rabbi. I have met him, and after speaking to him I was very impressed and felt he would be the right person to give leadership to the community. I wish him every success.

We also have Rabbi Lent with his wife and young children. He has been here in Dublin for the past few months. He was appointed to cater for the needs of the young children and I must say that already his position has been justified by the improvement in the Hebrew education of the children who attend his class.

# 9 Marriage and Family Life

I met my wife at a dance in Greenville Hall in 1940. The boys were on one side of the dance floor and the girls were on the other side. I saw this girl who was a total stranger to me. I went over and asked her to dance. That was the beginning of a romance that led to our marriage.

I danced with her many times during the evening and made an appointment to meet her a few days later. I invited her to a boxing contest in the National Stadium on the South Circular Road. She knew where it was because her grandmother lived opposite the Stadium. I still did not know who she was and I was surprised to hear that she was born in Dublin. She said that her name was Riv Baker. She told me her father was from Manchester and her mother was a Buchalter, a name I knew because the Buchalters were well known in the community. She wondered why I was called Nick, because her father said that Nick is not a Jewish name. I explained that my name was Nathan, but I was called Nick when I was at school and the name had stuck. We continued dating and after two years of courtship we decided to get married on 9 August 1942, the day after Riv's twenty-second birthday.

I remember our wedding day as if it was yesterday. When I woke up on that Sunday morning the day was dull and overcast. It was customary for the bride and groom to fast until the wedding ceremony was over. The hours passed and suddenly the sun began to shine and the clouds disappeared. The *chuppa* or marriage ceremony was due to take place at 2 pm at the Greenville Hall Synagogue around the corner from my home. I wore an evening suit of tails, white waistcoat and white tie. My brother Harry was acting as best man. He also wore an evening suit that was made in our factory.

We were collected to go to the *shul* at 1 pm. Although I could have walked there in five minutes I had to go by taxi. The taxis for Jewish weddings were supplied by Mr Mirrelson. He lived in Dufferin Avenue where he kept a number of taxis at the back of his house. I was surprised to see several of the factory staff outside the *shul* when we arrived. As we got out of the car they threw confetti at us and shouted greetings and good wishes. Riv got the same treatment when she arrived.

In the synagogue some officials of the committee were on the *bema* (where the reader conducts the service) and I was called up with Harry to sign forms relating to the marriage. In 1942, couples were obliged to have a civil marriage first and then have the religious ceremony. So I had to sign the register of the synagogue with Harry and two of the officials to witness the marriage. This situation was changed many years ago, and the synagogue can now register both the civil and the religious marriage. I think this also applies to Christian marriages.

When the signing of forms was completed, Harry and I took our places in front of the *bema* in the seats used by the President and officials during *Shabbos* services. By this time most of the guests and family members were assembled, including the Chief Rabbi, and the *mincha* (afternoon service) took place. Then, accompanied by Harry, my parents, Riv's mother, the Chief Rabbi and the Cantor, I stood in front of the Ark under the wedding canopy. A pianist (Mabel Fridjhon) played the traditional 'Here comes the bride'. Accompanied by her father, Riv made her way to the Ark and stood at my right hand side. I whispered to her 'You look lovely' and I saw my mother frown because you are not supposed to talk.

The Cantor began the marriage service and made the prayer over the wine. Riv's mother raised her veil and she sipped a little wine from the cup. I think my mother also held the cup to let Riv take a sip of wine later in the service. The Rabbi read the *Ketubah* (marriage vows) for the bridegroom and bride. Then I placed the ring on Riv's finger and the Rabbi said a prayer which I repeated after him. The final act is traditional at Jewish weddings, when a glass covered by a white cloth is placed on the floor to be crushed by the bridegroom.

The wedding reception was held in the large garden of Riv's home on Cowper Road. It was a very private affair with only the families present. We arranged to spend our honeymoon in Ashford Castle, Cong, Co. Mayo. Cong was about one hundred and twenty miles from Dublin, but the train took nearly ten hours to get there. It was just as well we had asked Annie Danker, who catered our wedding, to give us some food for the journey.

Ashford Castle is a lovely hotel, and in August 1942 many of the other guests were also on honeymoon. I remember that we made friends with Connie and George Sparks, a friendship that lasted long after we returned to Dublin. Noel Huggard looked after us very well in Ashford Castle. He was one of the Huggard family who owned a number of top class hotels in the west and south of Ireland. I remember the excellent food and beautiful surroundings. I also remember the games and dances that were organised for the guests. I won the table tennis competition, beating a priest who was staying in the hotel at the time.

The return journey from Cong was very slow, but this time it took a little less than ten hours. From Kingsbridge (now Heuston) Station we shared a horse and cab with a lady who lived in our area. This woman was much older than Riv and she proceeded to pour out her whole life story, while I just read the paper. This experience was repeated many times when we went on holidays, with total strangers confiding intimate details of their lives to Riv.

We lived with Riv's parents when we returned from our

honeymoon, as our house was not yet ready. One Sunday, about six weeks later, the two of us went to pick blackberries just outside the city and brought back jars of the berries for her mother to make jam. That night, Riv complained of having a bad headache. By Monday morning she was no better and the family doctor was called. He lived around the corner in Palmerston Road, and I recall that he came in to see Riv at least three times that day and again on the Tuesday. But the headaches got worse. On Wednesday there was still no improvement.

Early on the Thursday morning I looked out the window facing the street and saw a car drawing up. I noticed that Dr Nurock was talking to another person in the car. When both of them came up to the bedroom I learned that the other person was Professor Abrahamson. He pulled back the covers and ran a key along the sole of one of Riv's feet. He went downstairs immediately and rang for an ambulance to take her to the Portobello Nursing Home. He told us that Riv had meningitis. The word did not mean anything to me, but I knew the situation was serious.

Later that morning Professor Abrahamson was joined in the nursing home by Professor Harry Lee Parker, who I was told was a neurologist. They conferred together at the end of Riv's bed, not realising that she heard every word they were saying. Then I saw Professor Abrahamson pulling back the covers on the bed and Harry Lee Parker inserting a long needle to draw fluid from Riv's spine. She had been twisting and turning but this appeared to quieten her. The two doctors then left, saying they would be back later.

When they returned, I heard Professor Abrahamson saying to Harry Lee Parker 'We will take another lumbar puncture . . . the first one was negative . . . we have nothing to lose.' Professor Lee Parker inserted the needle into Riv's spine again, but this time she gave an unholy scream and I ran out of the Nursing Home with the scream still in my ears. When I came back after a short time, both doctors had left and Riv's father had arrived. He told me he had gone to the Greenville Hall Synagogue where they had the early morning service, to ask them to say prayers for his daughter. As is the custom in the Jewish religion, Riv was given a new Jewish name which means, according to ancient rites, that the person begins a new life.

At this time, Riv seemed to be sleeping. No visitors were allowed except myself and her father. Her mother had taken to bed in deep distress. I suggested to my father-in-law that he should go home for a while, and that when he returned I would go home to Cowper Road. I then lay back in the armchair and a strange feeling came over me. I heard a voice telling me that Riv was not going to die. Naturally, I didn't say anything about this to anyone. The next day I went to the synagogue before going to see her. I had first phoned for news and was told she had a quiet night. When I got to the Nursing Home, she appeared rested but tired after such an ordeal and told me a strange story

Riv said that my mother had visited her, had put her arms around her and said some kind of prayer. She had also told her to hold a red flannel cloth and put a small prayer book under the pillow. I was amazed at this story because I was sure that my mother wouldn't have known where the hospital was, even though it was not far from where she lived. I don't know how she got to Riv's room, as no visitors were allowed. Obviously nobody challenged her or there were no nurses around. It was a mystery for a while.

On Sunday when Professor Abrahamson called to see her, he was amazed at the transformation in his patient and said she could go home in a few days. Her father was delighted to see how well she looked when he came to see her in the evening. Before he left, Riv said to him, 'I hope the decorators are getting on with their work on our house.' This was a sure sign that she was on the road to recovery.

I went to visit my mother, and she told me that when she heard about Riv's illness she knew that she had an *inhora* (evil eye) from someone. She went to Rabbi Brown and wanted him to break the spell. My mother was a deeply religious woman, but she was also superstitious, believed in spells, and believed that the Rabbi's prayer was the way to break the spell. These ideas came with her and many of her kind when they came from Russia. Rabbi Brown gave her the red flannel to hold and told her to put the book, which was a *tillem* (book of proverbs) under the pillow to drive out the evil spell.

Leonard Abrahamson was very young when he came with his family from Russia to Northern Ireland. He attended the Abbey School run by the Christian Brothers in Newry, Co. Down, and in 1910 at the age of fourteen he won first place in all Ireland for Irish and Greek in the Intermediate Certificate. Two years later he won a Sizarship to Trinity College for four years, during which time he studied Irish and Hebrew. He also won a scholarship in modern languages (French and German). Then in 1915 he decided to study medicine, a decision which turned out to be very fortunate for Dublin.

When he was in Trinity, Leonard Abrahamson met Max Nurock, another brilliant Jewish student. The two young men became firm friends and Max brought his friend to the Nurock family home at 79 South Circular Road. There he met Max's sister Tillie and it was love at first sight. Leonard Abrahamson and Tillie Nurock were married in 1920. Max Nurock had an extraordinarily successful academic career and won a number of major academic prizes. He served with the British army during World War I and subsequently emigrated to Palestine where he played a major part in establishing the civil service. He was honoured later by the Israeli government when he was appointed Ambassador to Australia.

Leonard Abrahamson qualified as a doctor and then gained the higher degrees of Doctor of Medicine (MD) and Member of the Royal College of Physicians of Ireland (MRCPI). He was appointed firstly as Professor of Pharmacology and then of Medicine in the Royal College of Surgeons in Ireland. He became one of the leading physicians and cardiologists in Dublin, and in 1949 he was elected President of the Royal College of Physicians.

In addition to his professional work, Leonard Abrahamson played a leading part in the work of such bodies as the Jewish Representative Council, the Jewish Refugee Aid Committee and the Jewish National Fund. I had the privilege of hearing him speak at various meetings. He never had any notes and his delivery was so fluent that I was enthralled listening to him addressing the audience. It was no wonder that he was often called on to speak at weddings and other special occasions.

He was famous for his wit. There is a story told about an encounter with the well-known J. C. Flood BA, B.Comm., Barrister at Law, who also had post-graduate degrees in medicine and surgery. Abe — as he was fondly called by his friends and colleagues—had been treating a woman suffering from rheumatoid arthritis with injections of gold. After the patient's death he was presenting a paper about the beneficial effects of the gold injections. The audience applauded. Then Flood stood up and asked with heavy sarcasm if Abe had been able to recover the gold. Without a moment's hesitation Professor Abrahamson replied, 'Flood has more degrees than a thermometer without the same capacity for registering warmth.'

He was always in touch with the latest developments in medicine. An example of this is an interesting story that Joe Morrison told me. In 1930, Professor Abrahamson was treating Joe's sister Rose for rheumatic fever that had left her with a faulty valve in her heart. When she died in 1936, the Professor told the family that in future years it would be possible to replace faulty heart valves with new ones.

Tillie and Leonard Abrahamson had five children: Mervyn, Beth, Maurice, Max and David. Mervyn (everyone called him Muff)

followed in his father's footsteps. He became a physician with MD
and FRCPI after his name. He was Professor of Pharmacology at the
Royal College of Surgeons before he went to Israel in 1973. He settled
in Safed as head of the hospital there. Sadly, Muff died in Israel in
1993. Muff and his wife Marcia (Epsom) had three children, David,
Leonard and Leslie Ann. Leslie Ann lives in Israel. David, who
qualified as a computer scientist in Trinity College, married Hilary
Wine. He now lectures in computer science in TCD. He is also a
qualified engineer and pilot. He and Jonathan Moss—whom he
taught to fly—own a plane which they share. Leonard graduated in
electronic engineering in Trinity, but then chose to join his uncle
Mossie in the stockbroking firm of Solomons and Abrahamson. He
is married to Heather Waters.

Beth, the only daughter of Tillie and Professor Leonard
Abrahamson, married Ellard Eppel. Ellard is a doctor, and set up his
practice in the Crumlin and Kimmage area of the city. There was a
fast-growing population there, and he also had many Jewish patients.
He was a very caring doctor, much liked in the community, and in
due course he became President of the College of General Practi-
tioners. Beth immersed herself in community affairs and served for
some time as chairwoman of Ziona, a Jewish women's group. The
group prospered under her leadership and she had many loyal friends
and collaborators to carry on Ziona's charitable initiatives. Beth and
Ellard have four children, two sons and two daughters.

Maurice (known as Mossie) Abrahamson graduated in law and
was called to the Bar in 1949. But he chose to join the stockbroker's
firm of Edwin Solomons, which soon became Solomons and
Abrahamson. He served as President of the Dublin Stock Exchange
in 1961–62, the first time that a Jew attained this honour. His nephew
Leonard (son of Muff and Marcia) followed in his footsteps when he
in turn served as President of the Dublin Stock Exchange in 1993–4.
Mossie married Joyce Davis and they have four children, three

daughters and one son.

Max and David are twins. Max achieved the distinction of a scholarship in law in Trinity College. He qualified as a solicitor and became a leading international expert on the law relating to construction contracts. His work brings him to many parts of the world and his wife Edna often accompanies him on his travels. Max and Edna have three daughters and one son. David Abrahamson also studied in Trinity College. After qualifying as a veterinary surgeon he decided to study medicine, eventually specialising in psychiatry. He now lives in London and has two daughters.

When Riv had recovered fully from her illness, we moved into our first home. It was in Orwell Gardens, just off the Orwell Road, Rathgar, facing the river Dodder. It was quite a large house. Downstairs we had a good-sized lounge and dining room connected by folding doors, a large breakfast room and separate kitchen. Upstairs we had three large bedrooms and two small single rooms. There was a long back garden with two apple trees, a pear tree, a Victoria plum tree, two gooseberry bushes, a blackcurrant bush and a redcurrant bush, and a lawn. In later years, when our two children were growing up, I installed a large swing in the lawn area. Avril and Valerie enjoyed sharing this swing with their friends. The house had a front garden divided by a path leading to the front door. There was also a garage and a side entrance that I covered so that I could set up a workbench. Even though I had very little previous experience of gardening, I took pride in looking after our garden in Orwell Gardens. After a hard day's work in the factory I found it very relaxing. We had a rockery that always needed attention, and I planted all kinds of vegetables.

I was forever looking for ways to improve the house. I even found time to go to the Technical School once a week in the evening to learn how to use tools properly. I liked making things. I used to make drawings of what I wanted to make and then work out the measurements. My first piece of furniture was a bookcase with three shelves and sliding glass panels on the front. With my measurements, I went to Factor's sawmills, picked the timber that I needed for the bookcase, gave the measurements, called back the next day for my timber, and assembled the pieces. I put two coats of varnish on the wood. When the varnish was completely dry, I put in the plate glass panels that I had also bought made to measure. Then I was able to admire the first piece of furniture made by myself. I made many more pieces of furniture over the years.

Painting was something else that I enjoyed. I don't know how I found the time to do all these jobs, because I never neglected my business. I once painted the whole front of the house. It took me nearly two weeks to complete and while I was satisfied with the result I swore I would never undertake such an arduous job again. The most boring job of all was painting the front gate and railings. I also decided to make a path all around the long back garden. I didn't want to tackle it myself so I asked Alec Jordan, the foreman presser in my factory, if he could recommend somebody. Two days later he sent me a man with experience of building work.

I was not too impressed with the person who turned up. I explained what I wanted, told him I would supply all the materials, and asked him to give me a price. Without hesitation he said £100. I looked at him and said 'Are you crazy?' Then he said 'Would £50 do?' I asked him how long the job would take. He said it would take about three days. I asked him how much a week he earned and he answered '£6 or £7.' I told him that I would allow him four days to do the job and would pay him £4 and his meals. Without taking any time to consider my offer, he said 'That's grand.' I got a path that dipped in a few places, but it suited my purpose and I was able to walk around the garden in any weather.

In the early days of our marriage we were always able to have help in the house. Our first girl was called Chrissie, and she was with us when Avril was born in 1944 in Hatch Street Nursing Home. She came with me when I went to bring Riv and the new baby home. She held Avril in her arms and I remember admiring the thick black hair that Avril had when she was born. Chrissie stayed with us for several years and we gave her an excellent reference when she left.

A few weeks later, Riv had a phone call from a woman who had interviewed Chrissie for a position in her house. Riv gave her a glowing recommendation and when she put the phone down I asked what the other woman had said. She had asked Riv 'Are you Jewish?' When Riv answered 'Yes' she said she would never employ a girl who had worked for Jewish people, because we spoiled them. When I heard this I remarked 'What a pity you didn't say to that woman that we treat girls as human beings and feel  responsible for their welfare.'

Mary came to us before our second daughter, Valerie, was born in 1947. She was just as good as Chrissie and looked after Valerie as if she were her own child. I remember one sunny frosty morning when Mary took the children for a walk in the park across the river. They came back very soon and Mary was carrying Valerie in her arms. She told us that Valerie had slipped on some ice and her shoulder was hurting her. In fact it was dislocated, but because Mary had reported the incident so quickly we were able to have it put right immediately.

We lived in Orwell Gardens for many years, and we had very good and helpful neighbours on each side of us. We enjoyed hearing the sound of the river Dodder, especially after a storm, and there was a small waterfall just past our house. We spent many happy hours with the children catching 'pinkeens' with a small net attached to a long stick. I still remember the shrieks of excitement when one of them caught a 'pinkeen' or a tadpole.

In 1948 I bought my first car, a Ford Anglia. Before I collected it, my father-in-law gave me a driving lesson in his car. He made me start, stop, reverse and turn corners and after about two hours I was ready to drive. Next day, Monday, I went to the Smithfield Motor Company behind the Four Courts and collected my gleaming new black car, checked the gears and drove off through the traffic, full of confidence all the way home. Riv and the children were there to greet me when I arrived. We lived just past the bridge over the Dodder. You had to turn left off the main road and go down a steep hill to get to our house. Turning down the hill was not difficult but driving up the hill to the main road was a different kettle of fish. The problem was that you had to stop at the top of the hill to make sure the road was clear before driving on. It was some weeks before I could do this smoothly.

A few years later I bought Riv a secondhand Ford Anglia, gave her the keys and told her to go to Miss Eager for lessons. Miss Eager taught many Jewish people to drive at that time. I also told Riv that when she was ready to drive I would get her a new car. She learned quickly and it was not too long before I bought her a very sporty looking lemon-coloured Hillman Minx.

After the outbreak of war in 1939, travel and holidays outside Ireland virtually stopped, and people had to take their holidays in Ireland. Bray in Co. Wicklow was one of the favourite seaside resorts. It was only twelve miles from Dublin, but because there was a shortage of coal and the trains had to use alternative fuel the journey usually took over two hours. You could rent a bungalow in Bray from people who were delighted to get the extra money from families who wanted to holiday there. Greystones was another place you could go, but Bray being nearer to Dublin attracted more visitors.

There were many attractions for visitors to Bray. There was a splendid 'Prom' where mothers would watch the passers-by and gossip together. There was a bandstand where the Army No. 1 Band would give excellent concerts. There were also singers and Irish dancers to entertain people. There was a Punch and Judy show, and of course there was Dawson's Amusements Arcade at the base of Bray Head.

In the Amusements Arcade you could play Hoopla. This involved throwing rings over articles placed on a stand. Good judgement was needed to get the ring over the article, and if you succeeded you could keep it. There were dodgem cars in which young people raced around a circular arena and enjoyed bumping into each other. In the evening there was 'Housey Housey'—now called Bingo. This attracted mainly women. They were hooked to the game and many would sit playing every night. I remember there was occasionally a top prize of £10 to £20 for the first person to call 'Housey Housey'. Larger amounts of money may also have been offered. We often walked up to the Eagle's Nest at the top of Bray Head where there were Tea Rooms and sometimes dances at night. There were places where we could swim from a fairly long beach, with patches of sand here and there where children could build sand castles.

I think we rented our first bungalow for two months at £40 per month. The owner, a Miss Freestone, needed the extra money to supplement a very small income from her parents' investments. She was a charming lady and I am certain that she would never have let her house to strangers if she had other means of support. The letting arrangements between the summer visitors and the bungalow owners were based mainly on trust. No leases were drawn up but I never heard of any disputes. The people renting the bungalows usually looked after them as if they were their own.

We rented holiday bungalows in Bray for many years, continuing even after the war had ended. Some of the bungalows could have been bought for as little as £250 in the 1940s, but who could have had such foresight? Some years later, people began to buy bungalows in Brittas Bay in Co. Wicklow, and others at seaside locations in Co. Wexford. In many cases their children were able to enjoy these holiday homes when they themselves married and had children.

There were two *kosher* boarding houses in Bray at that time. One, run by Polly Stein, had been there for many years. Polly was a delightful person, warm and generous. She made everyone who stayed in her house more than welcome. She was to be seen every morning walking from her house on the seafront across the 'Prom' to the Baths to have her early morning dip in the sea. Polly also had a boarding house on the South Circular Road in Dublin, and catered there for people who wanted a *Shabbos* meal. Bluma Sharp started the other *kosher* boarding house in Bray, and it was very successful also.

While we were staying in Bray I used to swim nearly every day. On one occasion I was one of the few who braved a very high sea. It was full tide. I dived into the waves and began to bob up and down in the water as it was too rough to swim. I was enjoying myself thoroughly when I noticed that people watching from the beach were waving at me. I thought they were applauding my perform-ance, until I brushed some hair from my face and saw blood on my hands. I realised that I was bleeding badly from my forehead and swam in immediately to the beach, where I was given a towel to wrap around my head and brought to a doctor who happened to be nearby. He examined the wound and I had to have six stitches. He remarked that I was very lucky, because I must have hit a big stone as I dived into the waves and could easily have been knocked unconscious. I stopped diving into rough seas after that experience.

One evening in the 1950s Riv's father invited us to go to a greyhound race meeting with him. It was when my mother-in-law was away. My father-in-law enjoyed going to the greyhound track because it brought back memories of when he lived in Manchester. He was never a gambler and very seldom went to a meeting, but it was a lovely evening and he felt he would like to go to Shelbourne Park where the racing took place. Although I knew a number of Jewish men who had an interest in breeding and racing greyhounds, neither Riv nor I had ever been to 'the dogs'. Barney White was one of the people who owned a number of greyhounds. Max Bernstein also had a few dogs. I remember Max telling me that he received an offer of several thousand pounds for one of them after it won an important race. He refused the offer and ran the dog in a few more races with some success. But then there was a collision and his dog was injured. This ruined his chances of getting a good price for the greyhound, but as he said 'That's the chance you take.'

When we got to Shelbourne Park, Riv and I walked around. I had no interest in betting. We watched fascinated as the bets were placed, and watched races that lasted about half a minute. We saw so many people tearing up their losing tickets that I remarked to Riv 'These people work hard to make some money and then they go to the races to lose it all.' Then I saw Hymie Green. Hymie was a friend of mine and I knew he was a regular follower of 'the dogs'. I asked him for a tip. All he said was 'Back No. 4.' So I went over to a bookie and placed a bet on No. 4. We watched the race and saw dog No. 4 coming in a long way behind the winner.

I met Hymie again and said to him 'That wasn't a very a good tip you gave me.' He showed me the programme and pointed out that No. 4 had in fact won. I had no programme, and when I went to the bookie I had simply backed the fourth dog on his board. I went over to the bookie who took my bet. I knew him because he was a customer of my father and got his suits made in the factory. I said that he owed me some money, because I was told to bet No. 4 on the programme but had bet instead on No. 4 on his board. He asked me how much I had lost, and I said 'Two shillings.' He never said a word but reached into his bag, took out two shillings and just said 'Here's your two shillings. Do me a favour; keep away from me.' Hymie Green was very amused when I told him what had happened.

Both of our girls went to Alexandra to school and Avril continued for some years in Alexandra College where she showed great potential. We sent her to Bertha Weingreen for voice training. Elise Radnor and Anita Goldstone joined her. Avril went on to win the *Irish Independent* Cup for elocution. Naturally we were very proud of her, so we were completely shattered when Riv's sister Myra phoned to say that she had been taken into hospital in London, where she had gone for a holiday.

We flew over at once and went straight to the hospital, where the doctor treating her told us she had suffered an internal haemorrhage. She had been sedated and was comfortable, but she was still in a serious condition. We were taken to her room where she appeared to be sleeping comfortably. So we were totally unprepared for the telephone call next moring telling us that our daughter had died in her sleep. She was only eighteen.

We were stricken by grief. We stayed with Myra and Harold for the whole week of *shivah*. My eldest brother Sam came over for the funeral, along with my younger brother Louis. Sam and his wife Hetty had also suffered the tragic loss of a daughter. Their first child, Ruth, who was born after thirteen years of marriage, also died in hospital as a result of a haemorrhage after an operation to remove her tonsils. When we returned to Dublin many friends and family members came to the house to offer their condolences. But the death of a child is something one never gets over. As the years go by the loss becomes easier to bear, but even to this day it is very clear in our minds.

One day Marie Simmons told Riv about a new development of bungalows being built in Ardilea off the Roebuck Road in the Clonskeagh area. On the following Sunday, Riv, Valerie and I drove around to see them. What we saw convinced us that it was time to move after twenty-two years in Orwell Gardens. We moved into our new home in February 1964, and now that we are both in our eighties we are considering moving to an apartment within easy reach of friends, shops and transport, but we will be sad to leave the house and neighbourhood that we have enjoyed for over thirty years.

In 1965 Valerie spent nearly three months in South Africa. She stayed with the parents of Warick Ofsowitz, whom she got to know when he was studying medicine in Dublin. We received glowing letters telling us how much she was enjoying herself in Port Elizabeth. She also told us that she was driving a Mustang car and had a gun under her pillow at night. Another letter told us that Warick's mother was begging her to stay in South Africa, but she decided that she preferred life in Ireland and came home with wonderful memories of her holiday.

She settled down and got a position in an advertising agency in Dublin. However, it seemed that the yearning to travel was still there, so in 1968 she and a girl friend, Valerie Gross, decided to go to London and live there for a while. Valerie's work with another advertising agency brought her to Dublin on business from time to time. During one of these visits in 1971 she told us that that the young man she was seeing had asked her to marry him. His name was Gerald Moss. We went to London to meet him. When we met his parents for the first time we felt that we had known them for ages. The wedding took place in Dublin later that year. A large contingent of guests came from London and had a wonderful weekend. We made many trips to London over the years and on other occasions Valerie brought her children Dalia and Tasha to see us in Dublin.

The years passed. Dalia and Tasha went to school at the French Lycée Charles de Gaulle in London. Both became fluent in French and both learned Spanish later. Dalia spent a year at a well-known tennis school in Florida before graduating in History and Screen Studies at Clark University in Boston. Then she ran a company specialising in food supplements for people suffering from AIDS, HIV, and cancer. In her spare time, she and a friend wrote a film script which has been sold to a German film company. The film is a modern version of *Orpheus in the Underworld*. The most recent news from Dalia, now living and working in New York, is that she has left her job to devote herself full-time to writing scripts for television.

Tasha is an indefatigable traveller. Before going to Norwich to begin her university studies in American and English literature, she spent a year in Indonesia and Mexico looking after children whose parents were in jail. Currently she is running and teaching a diploma course for people involved in drugs awareness programmes in schools and colleges. She has spent a year travelling alone in Chile, Peru, Bolivia and Ecuador, occasionally giving English lessons to earn enough money to travel further.

She has also been in India for six months. When she was there she sent us a card showing the magnificent chandeliers in the Cochin Synagogue. This synagogue, built in 1568, is in an area of Cochin known as Jewtown where Jews lived happily alongside Hindus, Moslems and Christians. Now, there are only twenty or thirty Jews left. Many others have moved to Israel. As she travels from place to place, Tasha keeps in touch with her parents by email, and they pass on the news to us. She hopes and plans to work in radio in the future, but not before she does some more travelling. We received many cards from her from various places.

While we have two very ambitious granddaughters, now their mother is keping up with them. In August 2000 our daughter Valerie graduated at the age of fifty-three from Regent's College, London, with an advanced diploma in Existential Psychotherapy. We were thrilled at her success, all the more so since she had never taken the Leaving Certificate when she was in Alexandra College and never had any University degrees.

The course leading to her diploma was spread over a period of more than five years of lectures and intense study. Her interest began in 1989 when she took a course in psychology. Following this she worked for more than four years as a volunteer counsellor with Childline (a telephone helpline for children). She received the certificate of the UK Council for Psychotherapy, then decided that she wanted to go further and started on the five-year journey that resulted in her qualification as an Existential Psychotherapist. She now works with clients and families in one of the largest Mental Health Trusts in England, and also with some clients in her own home. The photograph we have at home of our daughter in her cap and gown gives us enormous pleasure. We are very proud of Valerie, and also of Dalia and Tasha.

# 10  In Business

In 1942, after an argument with my eldest brother, I decided to leave the family business. I rented two rooms in a building in Dame Street and did all kinds of work. I was able to get orders from some firms that I had built up relationships with while I was in the family business. But I never solicited any business from my father's customers. The first order I received from a warehouse was for 150 sports jackets. I didn't have a factory to manufacture the jackets myself, but I remembered that my father had a cutter who had set up a factory with the help of his two sons. I went to him and he was delighted to make up the sports jackets.

I was then in a position to take further orders from wholesalers, but I began to find it frustrating to have to tell him things that he should have known himself. I soon realised that while he knew about cutting he knew little about the actual tailoring of garments. I made a decision to start my own factory, as I had complete knowledge about making garments from the years I was in the business. I found premises in Pleasants Place where Adolf Baer had manufactured ladies' handbags, but he had moved to larger premises and the building was vacant. It was ideal for my requirements and Morry Gordon set up the factory with sewing machines and pressing machines. I owe Morry a great debt of gratitude for not insisting on immediate payment. He knew the background I came from and was not unduly worried about payment.

I decided to specialise in boys' and youths' garments and got the best possible patterns to manufacture the clothes. My brother Harry gave me great support when I was starting up. He was very friendly with Ronnie Mendelson, a pattern cutter who worked for Polikoff, an English clothing company that was set up in Rialto. At that time Polikoff were the best clothing manufacturers in Dublin. When I was setting up in the early 1940s it was boom time in the clothing business. The clothing trade was protected from imports, and Jewish firms dominated it by as much as 75 per cent. But the clothing manufacturers in the CMT business, that is cutting, making and trimming garments, were being squeezed out by the wholesalers and were being paid buttons for their work. I was kept busy. I had patterns made by Ronnie Mendelson, and when I showed the made-up garments the wholesalers were surprised and delighted with the suits I produced. Up to then, boys' garments had no style and not too much shape. I had a verbal agreement with the buyer of Arnott's wholesale department for their boys' suits and I also made a large proportion of their youths' suits.

I had good staff working in my factory. I was constantly urging them to try out their own ideas and was rewarded by their efforts. I think I was before my time in the clothing business. We were the first to try out new ways of making suits. We were the first to fuse canvas to the fronts of jackets. At the beginning the results were not good. But when we got a pressing machine that was adapted to fuse the canvas to the material the results were excellent. It meant that the tailors did not have to sew the canvas to the cloth by hand.

Then I began to use zips instead of the buttons and buttonholes for the fly on boys' pants. When I showed this to a buyer from Houston Morrow of William Street he was pleased, but said he was not paying anything extra for the making of the boys' suits. I told him there was no extra charge. It was, in fact, cheaper to insert the zip, as I was saving by not having to put buttonholes and buttons on the pants.

I began to get phone calls from owners of other factories. I remember a call from Mr Callanan who had a large factory making men's suits. He was asking about the fusing of canvas to the garments. I told him to send his cutter and tailor to us and we would demonstrate the whole operation. He then asked me if I minded showing our method to his men, and I replied, 'Mr Callanan, I don't want to be the only one using this method. People might think there must be something wrong with it if I was the only one doing it.'

We continued making other people's materials into suits, and being squeezed by buyers who would often say 'So-and-so are charging a few shillings less…' I decided to do something about it. I phoned John Macklin and Tom Marsh of Navan and suggested that we should meet in private in the Bodega Bar in Dame Street. The three of us were the largest of the CMT manufacturers and we knew each other, so there was no problem. I put forward a suggestion that we should decide what price we would charge for boys' and youths' suits, because the buyers were playing one of us against the other in order to get the price down. We could agree on a price and stick to it, and then if a buyer said that one or other of us had lower charges we would keep to the price we had agreed together. It was also agreed that each of us could try different ways to get a higher price, but wouldn't take less than the price we agreed between us. We were only protecting ourselves from being exploited by some buyers. There was plenty of work to be had, so we didn't have to be dictated to by the buyers. Our agreement worked very well and we arranged to meet once a month.

Then I introduced another scheme. I suggested that as the three of us were using the same lining and pocketing, we should buy in bulk. I got in touch with the salesman from Slane Manufacturing Company and asked him to quote for 1,000 pieces of lining, from which our three factories would draw supplies when needed. He was delighted to get such a large order and we were able to get four pence a yard off the original price. This was good, as between the boys' and youths' garments we were saving more than six pence per yard. With other bulk buying that we organised, it amounted to a big saving at the end of the year.

But we were still at the mercy of some buyers. One particular buyer in Houston Morrow said he wanted at least five shillings off the making of a boy's coat. He told me that another firm in Lower Abbey Street was selling a similar garment at five shillings lower and they had to match it. I was getting more than the price agreed with John Macklin and Tom Marsh, so I asked him would he share the difference. He refused, saying that they had to keep their margin up. I told him then that I wasn't interested in making the coats, even if the order was for 500 boys' coats. I also told him that I could have a good holiday with what I would lose on such an order.

I hadn't gone very far when I decided to manufacture my own materials. When I went to talk to my bank manager he said 'Nat, how much do you want? I'll support you because you are a man of your word.' I can't remember the amount I asked for, but it was more than sufficient for my needs without exceeding the overdraft. With the credit I got from the manufacturers, I started making my own brand of suits and carried on to the end of 1970. From then on I specialised in trousers.

In 1960 when the factory premises at 67 Pleasants Place became too small for my needs, I was able to purchase the leasehold of a derelict building nearby. Maurice Tolkin had used it for storing scrap and he no longer needed it. I built a warehouse on the plot of ground at 74 Pleasants Place, and as the walls were being put up I inserted into one of the cavity concrete blocks a short history of the area and of the Jewish presence in Camden Street from 1900 onwards. I wrote about how the Jews came to Dublin, noted where most of them came from and gave the number of Jews at the time. In the packet I also left some Irish coins from the half crown to the farthing in a sealed bag. I hope that one day, when the buildings in that area are demolished for some other kind of development, the bag that I put into the concrete block will be found and the contents revealed.

Every year I used to visit the main clothing exhibition, Imbex, in Earl's Court in London. I would just go for the day, to see how the fashions were changing. On one of these visits I noticed that nearly all the stands were displaying flared trousers. I became interested immediately. I saw the advantages of manufacturing trousers as against suits, including the fact that trousers would need so few trimmings. During the flight back to Dublin I began to formulate a plan to produce trousers. It was a momentous decision. This was in early 1970.

On the following Monday, I went to see Des Quinn, the buyer in Arnott's, and told him that I was manufacturing trousers. He gave me some materials to make samples, which I brought back the next day. He was completely satisfied and immediately supplied me with about ten rolls of cloth to start with. By Wednesday we were manufacturing men's flared trousers. Before the end of the week all the boys' and men's suits in the making were finished off and we changed over totally to manufacturing trousers.

I decided to manufacture trousers on a CMT basis to build up production and capital, and this is what we did for about six months. It was sheer pleasure not to be making suits. All that was required for the trousers was pocketing, waistband, and zips and buttons to match the materials. I got plenty of orders and started to plan manufacturing my own trousers. The break came when two young men approached me to make trousers for them. I saw the opportunity that I wanted.

I suggested that we form a limited company. They had already built up a connection in the country and I was already supplying some Dublin shops including Clerys. They accepted my proposal and I laid down stringent rules in the agreement. I had two companies: one for manufacturing the trousers and the other to wholesale the trousers to the shops. I made it clear that if they did anything underhand I would stop making trousers for the company that we named N. Harris and Associates Ltd. We adopted the trade name 'Grand Prix', we ordered size cards with the picture of a racing car on the front, and we got the name patented in my name. After about six months I felt unhappy with the arrangement. I got each one to resign from the company and made them sign letters of resignation that were prepared by my solicitor Don Buchalter.

From the moment I changed over from making boys' and youths' suits to manufacturing trousers, I was a happy man. All the machines that we had for making suits were used to make trousers, and I approached Morry Gordon for advice and suggestions as to what special machines were needed to boost production. Business was good, and when my yearly tax liability was assessed after a couple of years I was amazed at the amount of tax I had to pay. I said to my accountant 'Could I not share with my staff some or a lot of that money due to be paid to the Revenue? After all, my staff were responsible for making such profits.' He agreed, and I set about sharing the money with the entire staff. They were delighted to receive such an unexpected bonus. When I was asked why I was doing this, I said that I was not giving away my own money; if I did not give it to my staff I would have to give it to the Revenue. This happened in the early 1970s when profit sharing was unusual. I knew that what I was doing would ensure that I had a happy staff and improved production. They knew that the more trousers they produced the more money they would earn.

Around this time, I was in my office having my afternoon tea and biscuit at about 4 pm when I noticed two young children in the passageway at the side of my factory. They were going home from the school at the top of the street. I asked what they wanted and one of them said 'Mister, what do you make in there?' I said 'Trousers. Would you like to have a look around?' I took them around the factory, and they were very curious when I showed them a girl operating a button and buttonhole machine. I told them that when they grew up they could come and work for me. I then gave each of them a biscuit.

Next day, I had a visit from four children wanting biscuits. The numbers grew and I had to keep a small stock of biscuits to hand out. One day I noticed a little girl with her hand out. She had very bright eyes but a twisted smile on her face. What drew my attention to her was that her whole hand was turned back. I noticed her because I immediately identified her with one of my own granddaughters who was born with one half-arm, to just below the elbow. I made enquiries about the child and found that her name was Kathleen Rogers, she lived around the corner from the factory, and her father was not living at home.

I couldn't take that child's smile from my mind. I decided to pay a visit to her mother and to find out more about her. The mother told me that Kathleen was the youngest of three children. She was born with a cleft palate and the problem with her hand. The doctors operated on the cleft palate, but she was left with the twisted smile. When I asked about the child's hand, the mother became evasive and said that she was told to bring Kathleen back to the hospital when she was older. I felt that this couldn't be true. I had come across a few similar cases and treatment was usually started when the child was very young. Kathleen was already eight years old. I said that I knew some doctors in the Children's Hospital in Crumlin. I asked the mother if she would let me take the child to the hospital to have her hand examined and suggested that her older sister could come with her. She agreed to this.

I made an appointment and the three of us set off for Crumlin. After the surgeon had examined Kathleen's hand I asked him if anything could be done. He immediately said 'Yes, and the sooner the better.' I was delighted to hear him saying that. I explained who

I was and that I had no connection with the family. I said that the child was very bright and I wanted to give her a chance to have a normal life. I added that my company would bear any expenses involved. He said there was no need for that. I just had to pay £5 for the examination, so I wrote out a cheque for more as a donation to the hospital. We were given an admission date and told that Kathleen would have to stay for about a week. I said I would visit her each day and bring her mother to see her.

When I went on the day after she was admitted, I brought a few toys and some fruit and chocolates. She told me her mother and a sister had come to see her. The operation had not yet taken place, so I stayed for half an hour and then left. On my next visit I found that the operation had been done that morning. The poor child was very tearful, but her face lit up when I arrived with more goodies. Her arm was in a sling and her hand was bandaged. She didn't seem to be in pain. Her two sisters then came in. We stayed for a little while, until the nurse suggested that it was time for us to go, as Kathleen needed to rest. I drove her two sisters home.

I called again the next day and found Kathleen crying. She had a pain in her hand and had no visitors, not even her mother. I asked one of the nurses how the operation went. She said there was no problem, the hand was now straight, she would have to wear a plastic contraption for some time to keep it straight, and she could go home the following day. For some reason I was not free to take her home, so her mother arranged for a friend to do it. I asked her to tell Kathleen to call to the factory the next day. When she came in with the arm in a sling I impressed on her that she must keep it in the plastic support for as long as the doctors said. I also told her that she was to come in to see me each day for her biscuit and every Friday for her pocket money.

She kept to this routine until one day when I saw her on the street with her arm in the sling but not wearing the support. She saw me, but ran away when I called her. I phoned her school the next day and spoke to the head teacher. She had heard about my interest in the child and my efforts to help her. I explained that Kathleen must keep the support on all the time. The teacher had noticed that she wasn't wearing it and asked her why. The child replied that her mother said she could leave it off if it was hurting her. I asked the teacher to check each day to make sure that the support was kept on. Kathleen herself continued to ignore me and didn't come to the factory. The next thing I heard was that the family had gone to live in Skerries, a seaside town about sixteen miles from Dublin. At this point I could only hope that she was getting the proper attention to her hand, and as far as I was concerned my involvement was over.

Years later, I had a wonderful surprise one day when I brought a pair of shoes to my shoemaker for repairs. A young man took the shoes from me and said 'Hello, Mr Harris.' I hadn't a clue who he was. Then he told me that I used to give him biscuits when he and the other children were passing my factory after school. Immediately I remembered, and said 'What ever happened to Kathleen Rogers? She was one the children who got biscuits and she lived in Synge Street.' He replied straight away 'Oh, she has a great job working for some company and she drives a truck.' I asked about her arm and he said it was perfect. I smiled to myself at this happy ending to the story.

Joe Rubenstein was another person whom I was able to help when I had the factory in Pleasants Place. Joe was a dentist who found it very hard to adjust to retirement. I knew Joe well. If I were asked to describe him, I would say he was a 'Rubiner'. Saying that he was a 'Rubiner' meant that he was one of the Rubenstein family, one of the best known Jewish families in Dublin going back to the early part of the century. He was always a very energetic man, but now he felt lost because he had no other interests to occupy himself with. I met his wife Heide in Camden Street one day when I was still in business. She said she was finding it a problem to think of something for Joe to do with his time.

Later that day, on my way home from work, I called to their apartment in Palmerston Road and explained to Joe what he could do for me. I told him that we manufactured trousers and we needed to have some thousands of tickets printed for the production of the trousers. At that time we had a girl doing the printing. Joe's immediate reaction was that he wouldn't want to take the girl's job from her. I assured him that she would be delighted if somebody else would do the printing and let her do a more important job. He then undertook to do the printing that was done by hand, and I arranged to bring the bundles of tickets to have the sizes of the slacks stamped on them.

His stamping was meticulous and he was quick to tell me that he counted each bundle of tickets to make sure the printers were giving me the right quantity. He went on to say that some bundles were short of the number specified on the label, but other bundles had more, so they balanced out. Heide was delighted that I was able to keep Joe occupied. I emphasised to him that he did not have to print all the tickets in one day; he was to spread it over each week, as we had tickets already stamped for two weeks ahead. When I mentioned payment, he said 'How much have I to pay you? I am delighted to do the work.' But he appreciated the odd bottle of brandy or whiskey I gave him. I am happy to say that he was occupied for many months before he died. He was a lovely man and his kind is sorely missed.

My years in the business of manufacturing trousers were boom years for the trade in casual clothes. We were kept busy right up to the time when I decided that I had had enough. I remember arriving at the factory one morning in 1980. On an impulse I told my foreman and supervisor that I was closing down and everyone was now on redundancy. When I was in Camden Street later that day, I met a good friend and told him what I had done. He looked very concerned and said 'Is business bad?' I said 'I have never been busier and I don't owe anyone any money.'

I think the staff worked for nearly six months to make up the material we had in stock, and when the closing actually took place they organised a surprise for me and Riv. I was presented with a tea set and a beautiful fruit cake iced with the words 'Good health in your retirement.' Riv also received a lovely gift. When the staff had gone I still had the warehouse where the trousers were stored. It took another two years to complete the closing down. I had some offers for the company but could not come to a satisfactory arrangement. So I sold off my entire plant, and Morry Gordon bought back anything that was left over. I am glad to be able to say that any employee who was trained in my factory was able to get employment very quickly.

I enjoyed my last years in business, especially the last two years when Riv and I went visiting the customers in various parts of the country. They were sad that I had decided to retire and full of praise for the service they had received from the company. I know we had a very good reputation for delivery of orders because I always made sure we would never promise anything unless we were sure we could deliver. My motto was: 'Promise a day later and deliver a day earlier.'

Looking back, I think that changing over to manufacturing trousers and making up my mind to retire early were two excellent decisions. Cheap imports, that Irish manufacturers could not compete with, began to come in to Ireland in the early 1980s. I got in at the right time and I got out at the right time.

As I recall my own working life, I remember many others in the Jewish community who were building up businesses during those years. During World War II there was a serious shortage of textiles. Agents of textile manufacturers made great efforts to import as much as they could possibly get from abroad. At this time, Victor Enoch had a successful business producing an alternative to fresh eggs in powdered form. Then one day he received a letter from a girl he had known in London. She was now married and living in Argentina where her husband had an agency for a range of textiles. She wanted to know if Victor would be interested in having an agency for Ireland.

Victor knew that textiles were in very short supply and wasted no time in arranging with his friend to send samples of whatever was available. When he showed the samples his customers were delighted, and for the next few years he was kept very busy dealing with orders from all over the country. One day he got an order for knitting wool in various colours from a customer in Skibereen, Co. Cork. The Letter of Credit was set up and the goods were sent on a Greek cargo ship to Lisbon and onwards to Dublin with Irish Shipping. Shortly afterwards Victor was contacted by the customer who had ordered the wool. The wool had arrived but most of it was yellow! The various colours ordered were indicated by numbers, and it occurred to Victor that the censor might have changed the numbers in case they represented some kind of code. He told the customer to return the wool and he would reimburse whatever amount she had paid for it. When he hadn't heard from her after a few weeks he phoned to ask what had happened. She told him, 'It's all sold. Have you any more wool for me?' Victor said to me that he could see all the children in Skibereen looking like canaries.

The textiles agency was very hard work, but very rewarding. However, it was in the television rental business that Victor Enoch was particularly successful. In the late 1950s, TV was being relayed from Belfast to Dublin where 'fringe reception' was possible with the help of special aerials. Victor saw the potential for a TV rental business, and with the help of his sons Michael and Stephen he proceeded to set it up.

A shop was opened in Mary Street, and others soon followed. At first, the TV reception was dreadful. Some of the customers got nothing but 'snow' and each aerial had to be put in a special position to give a picture. It was a matter of trial and error, but gradually the reception improved. To receive BBC, UTV or Harlech TV from Wales, you had to place a high aerial, usually about fifteen feet, on the rooftop or in some other elevated position. People living at sea level had very poor reception.

One at a time, Michael and Stephen were sent to New York to train in the various aspects of the new business. As time went by, other firms were set up in Dublin. Some were cross-Channel companies that established branches around the town. Television began to be big business. Because he was very early in the rental sector, Victor—trading as 'Telerents'—had a distinct advantage. When RTE (the Irish national television service) opened on 1 January 1962, he was well placed to meet the subsequent increase in his business. He had the ability to pick good staff, he maintained strict control and he took great care to give his customers good service.

As the rental business continued to grow, more and more shops opened to take advantage of the demand. Then TV sets began to be imported from Japan. These sets were very well assembled and gave little or no trouble, so people started buying their own TVs. While hospitals continued to rent TV sets, there was a gradual fall-off in the rental sector, and Victor decided that the time was right to sell to the Smurfit Group.

The name Milofsky has been associated for many years with furniture making. The grandfather of the present generation started his factory in Jervis Lane off Capel Street. In 1975 the factory was moved to much larger premises in Mount Tallant Avenue. Five years later this factory building was set on fire—it seems that the target was an adjoining building owned by a British company. This particular company dealt in security devices, and the attackers were unable to break in. When they couldn't get into the British-owned building, they forced an entry next door and set the place alight with some of the timber and containers of glue they found.

The fire was a serious setback for the Milofskys, but being practical people they made decisions quickly. After his father's death, Ike Milofsky bought a shop in Harold's Cross where he started a DIY business. Following the fire, it was decided to go into the DIY business on a much bigger scale. The Harold's Cross shop was closed and the premises rented out. All the DIY stock was brought to Mount Tallant Avenue to be added to a larger range of goods. The building was divided into two sections: one to store a range of timbers and the other to be used as a machine room where the timbers were cut to size. The business quickly became known to the trade and customers appreciated the advice received from members of the family. It is now in the capable hands of Ike's son Kenneth and his cousin Michael.

The Caplins were also in the top class of furniture manufacturers. To this day, people are proud to say that they have Caplin furniture. Dave and Bertha Caplin had one son, David. He became a doctor and moved to England. Sons of other members of the Caplin family opened a DIY shop in Mary Street.

There were numerous retail furniture shops owned by Jewish people. These were mainly in the city centre. Eddie Barron had a shop on the corner of North Earl Street. Louis Levinson's was in Camden Street where Jack Zlotover's shop called The Star was situated. There was also a wholesale furniture warehouse in Cole's Lane off Henry Street.

I remember that at one time there were four shops on one side of Mary Street. They were actually beside each other and were owned by Harry Stein, Hymie Seligman, Judy Radner and Cass Baker. On the opposite side of the street there was one owned by Nat Fineman and another close by that belonged to a non-Jewish man called Broderick. Naturally there was competition between all these furniture shops, but generally speaking there was never any serious disagreement and occasionally there would be an amusing incident.

One of these was between Seligman and Broderick at a time when a stamped receipt had to be provided for any purchase over £2. Broderick must have run out of stamps and sent a boy with two shillings to ask Seligman if he would oblige him with twelve twopenny stamps. Hymie gave the boy twelve stamps. A few minutes later, Broderick strode across to Seligman's shop demanding to know why he had given used stamps to the boy. Seligman replied that he always put used stamps on receipts. Broderick then said 'But why did you keep the money for new stamps if you were giving me used stamps?' Seligman laughed, but he gave back the two shillings.

Leon's in Grafton Street was considered to be one of the top fashion shops in Dublin, after Doran's of Dawson Street. Mr Leon's daughters Ray and Ann looked after sales, with their father overseeing the entire business. Two other ladies' fashion shops were in Exchequer Street. Rosie Wine and Sally Citron were the owners of Femina's and Mrs Golding owned The French Shop.

An example of a completely different kind of business that I remember was Reuben Segal's manufacturing company, the Irish Jewellery and Metal Company. He worked with silver and silver plate and had contracts with the army and police force to supply badges and metal buttons for their uniforms. He built up his business gradually, starting with the first factory in Kevin Street, then moving to Harcourt Road and finally to Wood Street, where a factory owned by the Davis family who manufactured school garments had closed down. Two of his sons, Jack and Max, worked with him and they were joined later by Sid Morris who had married their eldest sister. Sid proved to be a great asset in the sales department. The Irish Jewellery and Metal Company was able to provide good employment and trained the men they employed for the intricate work. Reuben Segal was a very devout Jew, and was one of the stalwarts of the Greenville Hall *shul*. Jack was to follow his father in this respect and became President at a difficult time when the attendance at Greenville Hall began to decline.

During and after World War II, the Jewish community produced many entrepreneurs. One of them was Jack Restan. Jack was working for the well-known furniture firm of Millar and Beatty in Grafton Street. After some years there he was made redundant and needed to find other work. He was very interested in design and soon indentified a niche in the market where his talents could be used. He rented a small garage at the back of Dufferin Avenue for a few shillings a week and set about designing display stands. His designs were an immediate success and he soon had to move to larger premises off Rathgar Avenue. After a number of years he moved again, this time to his present location in Walkinstown.

Jack Restan has concentrated on designing stands for manufacturers to suit their particular products and his work can be found in more than twenty countries. What started as an idea became a reality. Success like that takes hard work and dedication to the creation of better and better designs as the demand continues to increase. He has been in his own very specialised business now for over forty years. There is surely a message in his success for young people with ideas today.

# 11 Community Service

When Robert Briscoe was elected Lord Mayor of Dublin in 1956 and subsequently went to New York for the traditional St Patrick's Day parade, the impact he made there was immense. Until that time many Americans were not even aware of the existence of a Jewish community in Ireland. When Bob Briscoe arrived, they were able to see and hear for themselves a Jew who was Lord Mayor of the capital city of a predominantly Catholic country. The interest he raised was tremendous and he made history again when he was elected Lord Mayor for the second time in 1961. Since the Irish Jewish Museum opened in 1985, visiting American Jews often ask 'Didn't you have a Jewish Lord Mayor in Dublin?' Many of them would be delighted to find that they were talking to Debbie Briscoe, Bob Briscoe's daughter-in-law, who is a member of the Museum Council.

American visitors to the museum are also intrigued when we show them the photograph of Ben Briscoe who was Lord Mayor of Dublin in 1988 and has been a member of Dáil Éireann (the Irish parliament) since 1965. It is a source of pride for the Jewish community of approximately 1,200 members that there were three Jewish TDs in the period 1991–7: Fianna Fáil TD Ben Briscoe, son of Bob, Labour TD Mervyn Taylor who also served as Minister for Equality and Law Reform, and Fine Gael TD Alan Shatter. Mervyn Taylor has retired from active politics, but Ben Briscoe and Alan Shatter continue to serve as members of the Dáil.

But to return to Bob Briscoe: he was very involved in the War of Independence on the Republican side, and he was a founder member of Fianna Fáil, the party established under the leadership of Éamon de Valera in 1926. He was elected to the Dáil in 1927 and held his seat until he retired in 1965. Since then the same seat has been held by his son Ben. Bob Briscoe died in 1969. He and his son Ben created a unique record between them by having an unbroken line of service in the Irish parliament for seventy-four years.

Bob Briscoe and his wife Lily had four sons and three daughters. Joan qualified as a doctor and then went to Canada where she practiced as consultant in respiratory medicine. Bill was a Sergeant Pilot in the Air Corps during the 'Emergency', then worked as a pilot with Aer Lingus and later with KLM. Joe qualified as a dentist in the Royal College of Surgeons and subsequently built up an extensive practice in Dublin, first in Baggot Street, then in Fitzwilliam Street and finally in Merrion Road. Brian is a radiologist in Baltimore, USA. Ben spent a short time in the Royal College of Surgeons before going into business and then into politics. I have never met Ida (who now lives in the USA) or Elise (who lives in England), but I once met Joan who was on a visit from her home in Canada. She was staying in Joe's house and I was very impressed by how well informed she was about all aspects of Irish life. I also remember Joe's mother, a tall and gracious woman who gave great support to her husband all during his political life but played no part in politics herself.

The four Briscoe boys learned to box at an early age and, during his brief period in the College of Surgeons, Ben became the British and Irish Universities lightweight champion. From an early age both Joe and Ben followed their father's example of commitment to public service in Ireland. Joe joined the LDF (Local Defence Force known later as the FCA) at the age of fifteen, when he was two years under age. He was attached to the 11$^{th}$ Field Medical Corps and served in the FCA for fifty years, while at the same time qualifying as a dentist and building up his professional practice. He carried the highest officer rank open to members of the FCA—Commandant—and his retirement at the age of sixty-five was marked by a special stand down parade in Cathal Brugha Barracks, Dublin.

Like his father before him, Joe saw no conflict between his commitment to Ireland and to his fellow Jews. Over the years he was regularly called on, in his capacity as public affairs spokesman for the Jewish Representative Council, to deal with various problems. Some of these were related to the ongoing conflict between Jews and Arabs. Because there was no Israeli Ambassador, Joe had to deal with media bias and in some cases to reply to adverse comments levelled against Israel. Very few people were aware of the valuable part played by Joe Briscoe up to the arrival of an Israeli Ambassador in Dublin in 1995. Most of the work he did could not be discussed in the community. Even since the appointment of the Ambassador, Joe has been called on for advice from time to time. The gratitude of the community is due to him for this, for his lifetime of service in so many ways, and for his ongoing contribution to The Jewish Home of Ireland.

After he qualified as a dentist in 1952, Joe went on a holiday to England with Stanley Buchalter who had qualified as a doctor. There he met and later married Debbie Black who was living with her family in Manchester. As soon as they had settled in Dublin where Joe established his practice, both Debbie and Joe began to take a serious interest in the community. This interest has continued to the present day. Debbie is involved in so many societies that it is hard to know where to start, but three of these are of particular importance at the present time: the Irish Council for Christians and Jews, the Jewish Museum Council, and the Ireland-Israel Friendship League (of which she is vice-Chairman).

Joe and Debbie have two sons, David and Daniel. Both of them are doctors. David and his family live in Boston. Daniel and his family live in Israel. Their parents can be proud of their two sons and of what they have achieved.

It was through the generosity of Mr and Mrs Potashnik that The Jewish Home of Ireland was established in 1950. They were visiting a hospital where a friend of theirs was recovering after an operation. This man was a very religious member of the Jewish community and it occurred to Mrs Potashnik that it would be wonderful to have a Home where Jewish people could convalesce after undergoing surgery. The idea did not leave her. She suggested to her husband that they should move to a smaller house and donate their large residence in Castlewood Avenue, Rathmines, to the Board of Guardians. Mr Potashnik agreed and the house was presented to the Board to be used as a Jewish convalescent home or nursing home.

The members of the Board of Guardians were delighted with such a generous gift, but because of the design of the house they felt that it would be difficult to use it as a Home. While they looked for more suitable premises, the house in Castlewood Avenue was rented out and the money received was put into a separate account. A special committee was set up headed by Solomon Verby, a very colourful character who devoted a lot of his time to charitable organisations. Two other members of that committee were Maurice Wine and Maurice Baum. Maurice Wine was a son-in-law of the Potashniks.

Around this time, the present property at Denmark Hill, off Leinster Road, Rathmines, came on the market. The committee decided that the house, owned by Harry Wine the antiques dealer, would be very suitable for a convalescent home, and then the idea of a retirement home was born. The house was bought and it was agreed to seek donations from the community.

When the news got around that there was to be a retirement home, many people were sceptical and said it would be too costly to maintain. But they didn't realise how determined the members of the committee were. Egged on by Solomon Verby, they displayed amazing energy in persuading the community to support their plan and in 1950 The Jewish Home in Ireland was ready for its first residents. The opening ceremony was a wonderful occasion for the committee whose combined efforts had been realised, and for Mr and Mrs Potashnik who saw their dream come true.

A fund was established and was supported by most people in the community. It continues to be supported to this day by grants, bequests, donations and other sources. Men from all sections of the community came together in the first committee and did Trojan work for the Home. A ladies' committee was also set up under the leadership of Fanny Turk, who was one of the Milofsky family. Some people thought that Fanny was a bit of a Tartar and many got the end of her tongue, but her main concern was the welfare of the residents and Fanny Turk got results. For the rest of her life she devoted most of her time to the Home.

Residents were expected to pay towards their keep, but the committee sometimes came across women or men who had no means at all. These people were taken also and received exactly the same treatment as those whose children donated money to the Home. Through their connection with the Board of Guardians, members of the Board of Management knew of people living in very poor circumstances. Some of them (especially the women) needed a lot of persuasion to move into the Home where they would have food, shelter and company. Even though they were alone, in one room with no heat and few possessions, they did not want to give up their privacy and independence.

On Friday nights and Saturday mornings there are services in the synagogue of the Home. They are attended by many of the residents and also by other members of the community. In the early days Louis Cohen looked after the synagogue, and he always made sure that there was someone to lead the service. I recall that his brother-in-law, Robert Isaacson, used to take the service on both days, although I cannot remember who it was that read the *Torah* on *Shabbos*. Myer Erlich took over the running of the synagogue after the death of Robert Isaacson. Myer had a rich baritone voice and sang many of the prayers he had learnt from *Chazzan* Garb.

Nowadays the synagogue is in the very capable hands of Norman Gruson, ably backed by Joe Briscoe and Solly Rhodes who is a resident of the Home and is in charge of all religious matters. Solly has a son who is a Rabbi living in Canada at present, where Solly visits him. I am pleased to say that I have often taken the Friday night service during the winter months when *Shabbos* begins in the early afternoon. Since Norman has been taking an interest in the Home he and Geoffrey Phillips share the services, with Geoffrey also reading the *Torah* and singing the *Musaph* service (the last part). I still read the *Haftorah* when I attend the service on Saturday.

Another member of the community, Laurence Citron, whose father Bert is a resident in the Home, has taken a leading interest in its management and has over the years improved the working conditions there. The Home has benefited from a devoted staff and an excellent Matron.

Geoffrey Phillips was born in Germany and was sent to England with the *Kinder* Transport (children's transport) in 1938. From 1943 to 1946 he served with the British army in Belgium, Holland and Germany. After the war he worked in the textile industry in Bradford, and in 1939 he met and married Phyllis. In 1950 he joined the firm of Stroud Riley, manufacturers of men's wool suitings. After some years with Stroud Riley in Bradford, he was asked to take charge of a manufacturing plant near Dublin where they produced similar materials. So Geoffrey, Phyllis and their three sons came to live in Ireland, and Geoff was managing director of the Dublin plant from 1951 to 1974. The Jewish community in Dublin was to benefit from Geoff's deep knowledge of Hebrew teaching, and the Jewish Home is indebted to him for his help with the services each week and for his occasional sermons on the *sedra*.

At one point there were four centenarians in the Home, including

Esther Hesselberg who was a resident for many years. Esther came originally from Cork. She was a very colourful character and gave many interviews for radio and TV. When Adelaide Road Synagogue closed, I alternated between going to the Terenure Synagogue and the Jewish Home for the service. On one *Shabbos* as I sat during the service in the *shul* of the Home I noticed a man who I assumed was a resident. As a few more people arrived I saw them going over to shake hands with him and saying 'Good *Shabbos*'. I then realised that he was blind. He was sitting in a relaxed position in a wheelchair and when he was called up for an *aliyah* (a prayer from the *Torah*) he was wheeled to the *bema* and read out the relevant prayer.

I found out that his name was Albert Coss, and at the end of the service I went over to him and said 'Good *Shabbos*; my name is Nick Harris.' He smiled and wished me the same. After that, whenever I attended the service in the Home I would say 'Good *Shabbos*, Albert, Nick here,' and he would reply 'Good *Shabbos*, Nick,' with a smile. Albert was in his ninety-ninth year and had been blind for only a few years as a result of trachoma. One morning when I wheeled him back to the dining room after the service, I met his wife. Millie was a very sprightly ninety-two-year-old, with bright eyes and manner. Before we sat down at the table, Albert kissed her and said 'Good *Shabbos*'.

I was anxious to know more about this couple and arranged to visit them in their room. There, Albert related the story of how he joined the British Army in 1915 in Leeds, where he was born. One day when he was on a message for his employers, an upholstery firm, he saw a large picture of General Kitchener pointing a finger at him as if to say 'We want you.' On an impulse he went to the recruiting office and joined up. He lied about his age which was only fifteen. He went to a training camp in Winchester for three months, and was then sent with a battalion to a town called Arras in France. He was there for a year. He said that the trenches were terrible but you got used to them. The winter months were awful, but there were periods when you could rest and have a cup of tea. He remembered a Christmas when the British and German soldiers stopped shooting for the day and shouted greetings to each other. But the next day it was back to shooting. After a year in the trenches it was discovered that he was under age. He was sent back to England but soon returned to France and the fighting. He had hazy memories of being moved from one place to another. When the war was over he stayed in the army for a further three years, and left in 1921.

After a variety of jobs, Albert opened a tailoring shop in Leeds. Then he was invited to go for a holiday to Belfast by his brother who had moved there at the end of the war. It was there that he met Millie, and it was love at first sight. When she refused to move to Leeds, Albert had no alternative but to move to Belfast. There were seven daughters and one son in the Leopold family and Millie was the youngest daughter. The Leopolds owned a ladies' garment factory, and when Albert married Millie he joined the family business. They enjoyed their life in a very close-knit community, and they had a daughter Rose who still lives in Belfast. They were delighted when Rose married a Belfast boy and presented them with a granddaughter, Amanda. When World War II broke out Albert was too old to enlist, so he served as a Sergeant Major with the Home Guard in Belfast.

In 1955 during a slump in the garment trade, Albert and Millie decided to move to Dublin where they lived for many years in a nice flat in Kenilworth Road. Albert had a job with Lillian Roberts, a ladies' manufacturing company, and according to Millie they were never happier. In 1997 they were forced to leave the flat following three burglaries in the space of two months, when Millie's jewellery was stolen and the place ransacked. They decided that they had had enough and went to live in The Jewish Home where many of the residents were friends of theirs.

Albert had never talked about his wartime experiences, even to

Millie or their daughter, so he was surprised to learn that the French government wanted to honour him as one of the soldiers who had seen action with the Allies in France during World War I. The Royal British Legion in Dublin had provided the French Embassy with information about Albert Coss, who was the last surviving soldier living in the Republic of Ireland. In January 1999 the French Ambassador, Henri de Coignac, came to the Home to present Albert with the Légion d'Honneur and to thank him for the part he had played in World War I.

Replying to the ambassador, Albert said how pleased he was with the decoration, even though it had taken them eighty-four years to make up their minds to give it to him! He felt that his Légion d'Honneur brought great honour to the Home and to the Jewish community in Dublin. When asked about his time in the trenches, he said 'I never gave it a thought until they all started asking me questions. Now everybody knows since I started spouting.' Sitting beside him, Millie talked about their marriage of sixty-six years and said in her Belfast accent, 'He is as good as gold. You wouldn't get many like him in a lucky bag.'

There was a big party in the Home to mark Albert's 100th birthday. There were many tributes and he replied in clear tones to every person who addressed him. One of the speakers was Ronnie Appleton, a well-known solicitor and spokesman for the Belfast community. When he said how pleased he was to see that Albert was still holding Millie's hand, Albert quipped that it was Millie who was holding his hand in case he went off with a blonde.

I was happy to know and befriend this wonderful man. He was always in good humour and never once complained about the loss of his sight. When I visited Millie to pay my respects after Albert's death, I couldn't help noticing the numerous family photographs on the wall facing her bed. I said, 'Millie, you will never be lonely with all the happy memories you have every time you open your eyes and look at those photographs.' Millie just smiled and held my hand, saying 'Bless you.' She died in January 2001.

It was in the early 1980s that I was invited to join The Sick and Indigent Roomkeepers' Society. It is a non-sectarian society and they wanted a member of the Jewish community in Dublin to be on the board of trustees. I was very flattered to be asked to join what was the oldest charitable society in Dublin. It was started in the year 1790 by eight men from various trades: a linen draper, two grocers, a carpenter, a stonecutter, a fruitman, a pawnbroker and a schoolmaster. These good men were appalled by the poverty and the miserable housing conditions they saw people living in and decided to set up an organisation to help them in some way.

In the early years the Society concentrated on the needs of desperately poor people in certain areas of Dublin. Each member of the Society agreed to subscribe two pence per week or eight shillings and eight pence per year, and they also set about encouraging their friends and associates to contribute to the fund. Soon, there were over eight hundred people giving money to this worthy cause. Various religious groups were invited to arrange Church collections, and this continues to the present day. As more money became available, more people were helped. In 1790, the Society helped 129 families, and the numbers increased dramatically during the following years. The Society has never been funded by the Government. Its entire income comes from donations and legacies.

The Sick and Indigent Roomkeepers' Society celebrated its bicentenary in 1990. Meetings had been held in 2 Palace Street beside Dublin Castle for nearly one hundred and fifty years. It was now found that these premises were no longer suitable for the work and new accommodation was found in Lower Leeson Street. The house in Palace Street was sold, but there is a preservation order on the front of the building and the words 'The Sick and Indigent Roomkeepers' Society' are still there to be seen.

What memories there are of those who worked there, of the people we interviewed, and of the harrowing stories we listened to before handing out assistance. I remember a young man who came in one morning when I was there. He told us that he lived in Canada but was visiting relatives in Dublin. He said that his mother had been helped by the Society when he was a child. He wanted to repay the kindness shown to her and he gave us $400. When the society moved to Lower Leeson Street it was clear that a different way had to be found to answer the many urgent appeals that came to us. We could no longer cope with the ever-increasing numbers of people needing relief, and it was decided to do the work through social workers, doctors, priests and hospitals.

I enjoyed my involvement with the society for well over twenty years and felt that I made a useful contribution to it. During my time, I proposed that a fairly large donation be given to charitable groups or organisations such as the Little Sisters of the Poor in Kilmainham. I had met some wonderful nuns who used to come to my factory for help, and we usually had a whip-around among the staff. The donation from the Society was used to help with the cost of installing a new lift and for necessary repairs in their Home for elderly men and women.

Some time later I was invited by the Mother Superior to visit the Home. I arrived about midday. In the dining room I saw each of the tables set out for lunch for four people with a white cloth and serviettes. In a recreation room I saw women sewing or knitting and men who were also occupied with some form of handwork. I told the Mother Superior that I could give her spools of thread of every colour; we were not using them because they were too small for our machines. Lining material to make carrier bags was something else that I was able to provide. I don't know what I expected to see during my visit, but I know that it made a great impression on me to see how the elderly people were looked after and how well-kept the Home was.

In addition to what we gave to the Little Sisters of the Poor, I proposed a substantial donation to Barnardos, and there were other groups that I suggested also. I was very gratified when a member proposed a very handsome donation to The Jewish Home in Dublin in my honour, in recognition of the part I played in the Society. I have not been active in the Society for some years, but I am still regarded as a member and receive minutes of the monthly meetings. I think I am now the oldest member of the Society.

I worked with some lovely people and was sad when they passed away. I made some wonderful friends and retain very good memories of the work. Today, the committee includes two retired doctors, a retired bank manager, and a retired Dáil deputy. While they will not be faced with the terrible conditions that prevailed in the 1790s, they are still aware of the need to help people caught in the poverty trap, they will continue to help them while funds permit, and no genuine case will be turned down.

The organisation known as B'nai B'rith was founded in New York during the mid-nineteenth century. There were thousands of Jewish immigrants in the city. They had left various countries in Europe to escape pogroms and persecution. Each of these countries had a different culture and a different way of life, with the result that there was a lot of disunity among the immigrants. In an effort to resolve this situation, a number of men from these countries got together. Their aim was to bring harmony to the many factions within the group, and they set up an organisation which they called B'nai B'rith.

The words B'nai B'rith mean 'Sons of the Covenant' and the new organisation sought ways and means to bring together the Jews living in New York. The movement slowly gained momentum and spread to other parts of the US where Jewish people settled. A charter was drawn up stating that the aims of the organisation were to promote charity, benevolence and brotherly love for all mankind.

B'nai B'rith began working in Dublin in 1953 and the motto 'To be of service' could be said to describe many of its activities. Its first President was Sam Scheps who came from Switzerland after the war. He started a business with Arthur Barling manufacturing ladies' clothing, and got involved in the community. Sam's brother Leslie came to Dublin later and married Sarah Baker. He went into the clothing factory owned by Baker's. I served as secretary of the group for many years and for a while as Vice-President. B'nai B'rith played an active part in the community and gave assistance in many ways to both Jews and non-Jews.

I remember a transport strike, and how we planned to organise a 'car lift' to the various hospitals around Dublin. There was an excellent response from our members and we brought many people to visit their loved ones in hospital on Sundays. Over the years, some of us used to take residents of The Jewish Home to visit friends or family, and many other members would recall experiences similar to mine.

I remember one occasion very clearly. This woman asked me to bring her to Grangegorman, a psychiatric hospital where her son was a patient. When we arrived she insisted that I accompany her, and I realised that it was her first visit there. We went in together and were directed to a large yard where we saw two groups of men walking around in circles. She went over to a young man who appeared to be in his early twenties and embraced him. The son didn't show any sign of recognising his mother, and after a short time we left. I felt very sorry for the mother. I offered to take her to see her son whenever she wanted to go, but she never took me up on my offer. I discovered later that the son was her only child.

The lady members of the B'nai B'rith helped in hospitals at Christmas time. Another involvement was with the Wheelchair Association when we provided people to assist those in wheelchairs on annual flag days. The jobs undertaken were very varied. They were practical, they were appreciated, and we were glad to be of service. But perhaps the most important project undertaken was to raise funds to provide a number of scholarships to schools attended by Jewish boys and girls. It was well known that Jewish boys had won scholarships donated to schools by non-Jewish past pupils. We wanted to show our appreciation of this by providing Jewish scholarships for non-Jewish pupils.

We solicited the help of the community and raised £5,000, which was a lot of money in those days. We then picked five schools for the scholarships: Wesley College, St Andrew's, High School, Synge Street CBS and Alexandra College. Stratford College was added to the list later. Then we had to decide on the amount of the scholarships and how to invest the money to fund them. By a large majority, we finally accepted Victor Enoch's suggestion that we should invest the money in Bank of Ireland shares. Another meeting was held to decide the amount that the investment would allow for each scholarship. Thirty pounds per scholarship was the sum decided. The secretary was instructed to write to the heads of the schools, informing them of our offer to provide the scholarship, the amount it was for, and stating that it was only to be awarded to non-Jewish pupils, and that the headmaster or headmistress had complete authority to decide who was to be the recipient. The only condition we made was that the award was to be called 'The B'nai B'rith Scholarship'. Thanks to the sound investment advice of Victor Enoch, the increase in the value of Bank of Ireland shares made it possible to increase the value of the scholarships in more recent years. I am glad to have been involved in the initiation of this worthwhile scheme.

# 12 Comings and Goings

The protective tariffs imposed by the government in 1932 made it possible for the clothing industry to survive and prosper. Without them, industry in Ireland could not have competed with the cheap goods that England could supply. Many Jewish-owned factories that were started took advantage of the protection, and even some English companies were set up in Ireland.

Polikoff opened a factory in Rialto and Abbey Clothing had a factory in Abbey Street. Dubtex, which was in existence before World War I, had a factory on Wellington Quay where they produced excellent men's clothing. I remember that they were the first in Ireland to introduce self-supporting sports trousers and I saved up to buy a pair. I think the price I paid in 1932 was twelve shillings and sixpence. Dubtex was owned by three brothers, Solly, Pat and George White. Solly was in charge of administration, Pat was in charge of the factory, and George had the key role of selling and travelling. They made a very effective team.

Automac, owned by the Davis family, had a factory making caps and school uniforms. The Bakers also had a factory in Chancery Street near the Four Courts making boys' and youths' clothing. Resnicks, Sabins, Whyte Brothers and ourselves had men's clothing factories. There were many ladies' clothing factories also, and furriers like Nat Mendel, Alfred Bloom and Taylor Vard. All these people helped to build the economy of the country and employed hundreds of Irish men and women.

During the 1930s, Jewish people living in Germany and Austria were aware of increasing anti-Semitism and they began to leave.

Some came to Dublin. They came with few possessions and had left good businesses behind them. Among the first of these to arrive in Dublin were Adolf Baer with his wife and son. Adolf had a factory manufacturing ladies' handbags in Germany. When he saw signs of trouble early in the 1930s, he quietly set about taking designs of the handbags and brought them with him when he came to Dublin. He was a very enterprising man and soon after his arrival here he began to look for backers to set up a manufacturing plant. No ladies' handbags were being manufactured in Ireland at that time. It didn't take long for Monty Buchalter and Jack Zlotover to see the possibilities in such a project, and a company was formed with the three of them as directors.

Jack Zlotover owned the Star Furnishing Company in Camden Street. It happened that there was a large vacant site behind the shop. Monty's wife Sarah owned the building. A factory was built in a very short time and Adolf Baer began manufacturing handbags— in premises blessed by the Archbishop of Dublin. The business prospered to such an extent that Adolf decided to move to much larger premises in Pearse Street in 1942.

Adolf's wife died some years after coming to Dublin. His second wife was Doreen Isaacs, whose sister Ruby was married to my brother Hymie. They had a wonderful marriage for many years. Adolf had a son who qualified as a doctor and then emigrated. Adolf and Doreen continued the business until he retired. After he retired, Solly Moher, who had been one of his trainees, opened a handbag factory just off Clanbrassil Street, with the financial help of Simon Taylor.

The three Witztum brothers, Marcus, Arnold and Nathan, arrived from Vienna. Nathan married Mabel Fridjhon, a very accomplished pianist who played at many concerts and weddings. Arnold married a charming girl from Belfast, a wonderful and very caring person who endeared herself to the community. Sadly, Eileen and Arnold are no longer with us. They had one daughter Anna, who is married to Norman Adler.

The Witztums started manufacturing ladies' wool garments, using their own woven fabrics. This had not been done before in Ireland. Other Jewish people who came here from Europe also set up new industries. The Hirsch family started a ribbon factory in Galway. A hat factory was also opened in Galway. Men's braces were made by a Mr Margolis.

Mr Margolis arrived from Germany around 1934. He came by himself to try to set up in business, so that he could bring his wife and children over to Ireland. I came home from synagogue one Friday evening and found him in our house. My brother Harry had met him and brought him home for dinner. This was not unusual. Jewish families welcomed many of the refugees who managed to come to Dublin. Mr Margolis told me that he had a belt factory and also manufactured men's braces in Germany, but had to leave as conditions were getting bad. I asked him for a sample of his braces, which he gave me. On the Monday morning I brought the sample braces to a friend of mine who was a buyer in Callanan & Company, warehousemen. He gave me a starting order for twelve gross pairs of the braces. Naturally, Mr Margolis was very happy with the order and he managed to set himself up in a small work-room to manufacture the braces. I also introduced him to Ferrier Pollock's, another warehouse in South William Street.

Mr Margolis built up an excellent business and was able to bring his whole family to Dublin. Incidentally, he employed a Mr Model as a traveller. This was Philip Model who married one of the Margolis girls, and who later became choirmaster in Adelaide Road Synagogue. I refused to take any commission for the orders that Mr Margolis got from Callanan's or from Ferrier Pollock's.

I also became involved in another situation when I came home one day and found a Mr Wyshniak there. He became friendly with our family and one day he asked if I would help him to get his daughter out of Hungary, where she had gone from Germany. After some discussion, I went with him to the Hungarian Embassy. I was to say that I was engaged to his daughter Sabina. I spoke to the Ambassador. I told him that I was engaged to Sabina and asked him if he could help me to get her out of Hungary. I don't know whether he believed me or not, but he issued a visa for Sabina to come to Ireland, which she did soon afterwards.

Sabina settled down with her father. She met and married Monty Shortts who had come over from London. He was a furrier and had a shop or rooms in Capel Street. I don't think I met Sabina more than a few times after she came to Dublin. I know that Monty died. He was a nice man, and I often wondered if he knew what part I played in bringing his wife to Ireland.

Many people, Jewish and non-Jewish, left Britain for Ireland in the years before the outbreak of World War II. Many had Irish connections. Most of them were highly skilled tradesmen. They either joined a company or set up in business for themselves. In our own factory we employed two brothers named Greene who improved the quality of the men's suits we were manufacturing.

These newcomers also set up a social club in Harcourt Street, next to the High School. It was called The Silver Slipper. Dances were held there every week and the club became a very popular meeting place for members of the community. There was another social club that had been started much earlier in Harrington Street—in the late 1920s. It was called the Jewish Literary Club even though the only papers brought into the club were newspapers.

A number of men decided that they wanted a place where they could go for a relaxed evening after work. Harrington Street was within walking distance for members. The club was often referred to as the 'illiterate' club for men only. They had a reading room and a full sized billiard table that was in constant use. There was also a card room where they could have light refreshments served to them by Norman Green. But no alcohol was served. The Literary Club was used mostly by married men who knew they would always meet some of their cronies for a chat, but I can't remember ever hearing that they had a visiting speaker.

The club came into its own during the war years when transport was limited and many a deal, good and bad, was struck between the members. I'm not too certain when the club closed. It may have been during 1950. It served an excellent purpose while it was there, and I'm sure that many a tale could be told by some of the former members. I was never a member but my late father-in-law, Cass Baker, usually visited the club with Louis Levinson once a week to play a game of billiards. He often played with Nandor Freilich who was the Cantor of Adelaide Road Synagogue. He once told me about a game of billiards he had with another member of the club. He accidentally potted his opponent's ball into one of the pockets of the table. The opponent was known to have a short temper and reacted by making a swipe at him with a billiard cue. Fortunately he missed, but my father-in-law was sure that he meant to hit him. He took great care not to play with that man again.

Many of those who came from England married local girls. I remember seeing Leon Brandon in our house soon after he arrived. He was a ladies' hairdresser and stylist. My brother Hymie was getting married to Ruby Isaacs. My mother and sisters were getting ready for the wedding and Leon was helping them with their hair. He was a charming man and full of personality. He married Lena Spiro. She helped him to set up a salon in South King Street which became one of the leading hairdressers in Dublin.

With the approach of war, there was increasing concern for the safety of Jewish people who wanted to come to Ireland. In common with many other countries, the Irish policy towards aliens and refugees was restrictive, possibly because of the high rate of unemployment, and many who were refused admission died later in the Holocaust.

In 1995, the Taoiseach, John Bruton, spoke in Terenure Synagogue at a ceremony commemorating the fiftieth anniversary of the liberation of Bergen-Belsen. He recognised that Ireland's doors 'were not freely open to those families and individuals fleeing from persecution and death' and said, 'We must acknowledge the consequences of this indifference.'

While many had relatives who died in the Holocaust, Ettie Steinberg was the only member of the Dublin Jewish community to be killed by the Nazis in a concentration camp. She and her husband and their three-year-old son died in Auschwitz in September 1942. Ettie and her little boy were also the only Irish citizens to die in the Holocaust. Together with the rest of my family I was at Ettie's wedding in Greenville Hall in July 1937. It was a joyous occasion, full of Jewish ritual and tradition. It was felt that Ettie had made a good *shiddach*. She was a lovely girl and everyone was happy for her. Her husband, Vogtseck Gluck, belonged to a very orthodox family of goldsmiths in Belgium, and he worked in the family business in Antwerp.

Ettie and her husband settled down in Belgium, but not for long. The news coming from Germany was very worrying. They moved to France and their son Leon was born in Paris in March 1939. Ettie's family in Dublin was very concerned for her safety, even though they continued to receive letters from her. When the letters stopped and a letter from her brother was returned, they were frantic for news of their children's whereabouts. I can still remember the sadness in the entire Jewish community when the Belgian Embassy informed the family that Ettie, her husband and son had been transported to Auschwitz and murdered. Scores of people visited the home of the Steinbergs as they sat *shivah* for their daughter, their grandson and their son-in-law.

Bertha and Jack Weingreen should be remembered and honoured for the work and effort they made to get children out of the notorious concentration camps in Poland and Germany. They actually went into the camps to do what they could to help those unfortunate people. There were some lucky children whose parents managed to send them out of Germany just before the war. Some of these children came to Dublin and were put up in Jewish homes. Later the children were sent by train to Belfast where the Mill Isle Camp was set up for the refugee children.

Two other children, Susi Diamond and her brother Terry, were brought to Ireland from Belsen by Dr Robert Collis. They were adopted by Willy and Elsie Samuels who had no children of their own and I am pleased to say that they both had a wonderful upbringing and are still living in Dublin. Terry has given many interviews of his harrowing memories of the camp he was in, and the inhuman attitude of the camp soldiers They will always live with him.

In May 1945, when the war was finally over in Europe, people all over the world were shocked at the pictures shown of concentration camps. In Dublin, the feeling was very much the same. We Jews, living in a neutral country, had been able to live our lives in comparative comfort, without knowing what was really going on. Ireland had been under very strict censorship and even news of the progress of the war was not fully reported.

However, Dublin Jewry quickly got down to the task of helping the thousands of children orphaned and homeless. At last they could do something.

A Jewish Children's Rescue Fund was opened in May 1945,under the able Chairmanship of Dr Bethel Solomons, with Victor Waddington as Vice-Chairman, Morris Ellis PC as Hon. Treasurer, and Dudley Newmark as Hon. Secretary, and a most willing committee of over twenty men and women from all the various societies wanting to help.

The fund was to be for six months, but it did not close until 11

December 1945 and the subscription list was not fully completed until early 1946. There was a massive response from the community as if each and every person felt a guilt that they wished to purge, so they gave generously, even non-Jews responded to such a worthy cause. Many fund-raising functions were held including cinema shows, dinner dances and art auctions. A grand total of £20,000 was collected and the expenses came to a mere £74 for printing and postage. No money was wasted. It was arranged that our help in the work of rescue and rehabilitation would be administered through proved organisations, each one to give a guarantee to the Dublin group that the fund received from them would be used in connection with the work for children only.

At the beginning of the war, there was a lot of talk about Ireland being a hotbed of German spies. I remember one particular incident. My father always had a number of private customers, and one day before the war a man came to the factory to have a couple of suits made. I was the one who usually took the details of private orders, so I proceeded to take this customer's measurements. I had never met him before but he gave me the impression that he knew my father. I thought nothing more about it until two people came to the factory one day to ask questions about this man, who turned out to be a German. They were from the Aliens Department and wanted me to show them the book in which I entered the measurements and took note of the customer's name. They asked if he was interested in making sure that the suits fitted him well. Did he want them easy fitting? Did he give any indication as to how the suits should be made? They appeared to be satisfied with my answers. I am not certain of the man's name but I remember that he lived on the Templeogue Road.

One way or another, the war brought many changes to the way of life of everyone living in Ireland. The country was very dependent on imports and rationing was introduced. The use of motorcars was affected first, when coupons were issued for petrol and oil. Then, for a while, there were gas bags on the top of cars and engines were adjusted to take the gas. Even the gas was rationed. The petrol shortage caused many Jewish people to lose a business they had developed before the war. They used to sell clothing, blankets, etc. to customers living on small farms in remote areas outside Dublin. Without motorcars they had no way of reaching these farms.

Imports of coal virtually stopped and we had to use blocks of wood and turf for heating. Fortunately, there was an abundance of turf. I am sure there are many people who remember seeing the very big turf banks set up in Phoenix Park where people were able to purchase turf. It was lucky also that our factory was next door to O'Dea's bedding factory. O'Dea's made bedroom furniture and we were allowed to take enough timber cuttings to keep our boiler going. We also had an allocation of Irish anthracite. Even the train engines had to use anthracite and blocks of wood. With this kind of fuel, the twelve-mile journey to Bray took nearly two hours.

Max Berber should be remembered by anyone who had to cope with wartime shortages in the manufacturing trade. Max had a small warehouse in the North Lotts that ran between Bachelor's Walk and Middle Abbey Street. He also had a small factory making boys' pants. In the early part of the war his warehouse stocked a variety of items ranging from buttons to piece goods. He also had quotas for linings and trimmings. People got to know about the stocks he carried and when shortages began they would get patterns and samples from Max Berber and offer the goods to various factories.

In many cases, the people who took the samples of material and sold the goods were not able to pay Max until they were paid by the purchaser. Max gave them the goods and told them they could pay him when they themselves were paid. Many of the people who eventually settled in Dublin and married local girls earned their living in this way through the generosity of Max Berber.

His brother-in-law, Joe Jay, came from Glasgow to join Max in the business. Joe endeared himself to the Dublin community and became very involved in the Scout movement. Max and his wife had two children, Manie and Stanley. Manie went on to qualify as a doctor and married Marie Walsman. Unfortunately he died at a very young age. Marie Berber's sister Edna married Max Abrahamson.

During the war years my brother-in-law, Sam Farbenbloom, who was married to my sister Leah, built up a thriving business in the export of rabbit skins to Belgium and rabbit meat to the Smithfield Market in London. In the late 1930s an Englishman called Davidson had started a company in Dublin called Fur Dyers and was exporting rabbit skins and meat. At the same time Sam had vegetable shops in Rialto and in Crumlin and a shop in Ranelagh where he sold fish, chickens and some rabbits. He contacted Mr Davidson to explore the possibility of buying more rabbits. He must have made a good impression because he was invited to join Fur Dyers. Under his management the business began to expand, so he got out of the shop in Ranelagh and devoted all of his time to the new venture.

Fur Dyers soon became the largest exporters of rabbits from the Republic of Ireland. Depots were opened for people to send the rabbits by rail to Fur Dyers in Dublin. Sam asked my brother Harry to go to Ballina, Co. Mayo to open a depot and buy rabbit skins to send to Dublin. Harry did this and soon built up a thriving business with the rabbit skins.

Soon Harry became a well-known person in the town and joined the local golf club. He had never played golf before, nor had he taken part in any sporting activities. He became addicted to the game and in his second year playing golf he won the Captain's Prize. The third year he won the President's Prize and then he lost the business by neglect. When Harry returned to Dublin, he went back to the family business, and later joined Edmondstown Golf Club where he was an accomplished player.

Fur Dyers' business was booming and Sam was handling vast amounts of money. With the threat of war looming he bought a house in Clonmel, Co. Tipperary. He was afraid that Dublin would be bombed and decided to move his wife and three children to a safer area. When it became clear that Ireland would remain neutral, the family moved back to Dublin to a beautiful home in Palmerston Park.

When I met my good friend Joe Morrison recently, he told me an interesting story about how he and his brother Dave became involved in the rabbit export business in Limerick, and about their links with Sam Farbenbloom. He also told me about the impression made on the people of Limerick by his father's funeral in 1930. It was attended by a large number of non-Jewish people who were anxious to see a Jewish funeral. The last Jewish funeral in Limerick had taken place in 1898. One reason for the large attendance of non-Jews was the belief that Jews were buried standing up, and they wanted to see for themselves if this was true!

When Dave was visiting Dublin during 1940, he met Jack Jascourt who had been in Fur Dyers but was now working with Abe Stein collecting and exporting rabbit skins. Jack suggested to Dave that he should set up a store in Limerick and start collecting rabbits. The proposal came at a time when the brothers were looking for an alternative to the business they had had to abandon because petrol was rationed and they couldn't carry on without a car. So the idea of going into the rabbit business appealed to them. They were joined by Bob Taylor from Dublin who was similarly affected by the petrol shortage. Bob's father happened to have a store in Limerick that they were able to use.

They set up a company and the word got around very quickly that they were paying good money for rabbits. They bought a two-ton lorry and got the engine converted to use coal. They built up a big business, exporting the skins to Belgium and the meat to London where there was a man named McKeever in the Smithfield Market who took all the rabbits they could send. They also rented a cold storage plant from the Limerick Steam Shipping Company where they were able to store the rabbits prior to export. As the business expanded, Ike Lentin from Limerick took an interest in the firm. They agreed to sell the skins to Ike's father who had set up an export company of his own, and Joe's company concentrated on exporting the rabbit meat.

They ran into trouble when they were told by the Limerick Steam Shipping Company that they could no longer store the skinned rabbits. Joe immediately got in touch with his solicitor, Victor Elyan, to take out an injunction against the company with which they had a verbal agreement. They won the case in Court, with an apology from the shipping company and an agreement to continue storing the rabbit meat.

Shortly after this, Bob Taylor left the company and went back to Dublin to get married to Naomi Engelman. At the same time Ike Lentin sold his interest to Fur Dyers and Joe and Dave decided to do the same. They contacted Sam Farbenbloom and a deal was struck. The ship carrying their last consignment of eight boxes of rabbit meat to McKeever in London was torpedoed by a German submarine. Fortunately they were covered by an export insurance scheme set up by the Irish government and received full compensation. Joe and Dave moved from Limerick to Dublin in 1944. Joe married Cleo Wine and Dave married Mary Hodes from Belfast.

In the meantime, more and more people were going into the business of exporting rabbit meat and skins. By 1945 the market for rabbit meat was slowing down and the demand for rabbit skins collapsed. A few years later Sam Farbenbloom and my sister moved to London with their seven children. Sylvia, their eldest daughter, entered the London Jewish Hospital to train as a nurse. After some time in London, all the other children went with their parents to

Israel where immigration was being actively encouraged.

But before they left their London home, there was a knock on the door one day. Sylvia was on a break from the hospital. With her hair in curlers, she opened the door to an American soldier. His name was Ronnie Weiss. He had met Sylvia's brother Frank somewhere, and Frank told him that if he ever got to London he should call to the family home for a good *kosher* meal. Ronnie and Sylvia married some months later when Sylvia qualified as a nurse. She joined Ronnie when he returned to the US and they and their three sons now live in Los Angeles.

After moving to Israel, the Farbenbloom family settled down on a kibbutz. The children quickly got jobs outside the kibbutz, but Sam and Leah decided to make the kibbutz their home. Sam started a chicken farm that became a valuable asset. Leah also took up a position on the kibbutz and both of them led a contented life. When Sam died, a plaque in his memory was erected in the kibbutz. They had an exciting life when they were in business in Dublin, but I don't think they had any regrets.

Sam had managed to bring his brother Benny over from Czechoslovakia just before the war. He went to work at once in Fur Dyers, and proved to be both capable and reliable. When Sam and his family left Dublin, Benny did not go with them. He had saved money earned from the business and took some time off to plan what he wanted to do next.

He had contacts with a lot of shopkeepers in the country who used to send rabbit skins to Fur Dyers by rail. So he decided to buy a van and bring them supplies of fruit and certain vegetables from the Dublin Fruit Market on a regular basis. Before starting he visited shops that were located mainly along the East coast, and got to know what they wanted. The business went very well and soon expanded into other areas, with the result that Benny had to invest in a much bigger van.

He approached me and we discussed the situation. I told him that he would have to get accommodation from the bank where he had his account, and I went with him to the branch at Kimmage Cross. My own account was with the Dame Street branch of the same bank. I offered to go as guarantor for Benny, but the manager agreed to give him an overdraft without my guarantee. In the manager's presence, I explained to Benny that if he ever had a problem with repayments he must phone the bank and tell them when he would be able to pay. This was important in Benny's case because he couldn't pay the bank until his customers paid him.

Then I organised Benny's arrangements with suppliers in the Fruit and Vegetable Market. His brother had dealt with a number of them in the past. Some of them spoke highly of Sam but others were not too enthusiastic. So for quite a while Benny had to pay cash for his supplies. This meant that he had to carry as much as a few thousand pounds in cash. At the end of the first year, I suggested that it was time to change this arrangement and went with him to his largest supplier, McNulty. Benny offered to pay by cash or by cheque—he had the cash in one hand and a cheque in the other. McNulty said that he didn't want cash lying around and would be delighted to accept a cheque. After this, all the other merchants also accepted Benny's cheques.

Benny was a boarder in the Kenilworth Park home of Mrs Harriman, a widow with two children. From time to time, he would tell me that he had been approached by a certain person with regard to meeting a girl with a view to marriage. Then Mrs Harriman's son got married and not long afterwards her daughter also married, leaving Benny living alone with the mother. When this became known some of the more religious members of the community became concerned, and they proposed that Benny should marry Gertie Harriman. I was very enthusiastic about this. I pointed out that he had lived in this house for over ten years, that they knew each others' likes and dislikes, that he got on well with the children, and that the children were very supportive of the idea of the marriage. I said that the main thing was to be sure that he liked the idea, because all he would be doing was moving from one room to another.

The date was set for the marriage, and then Benny came to me to say he had a problem. When he arrived in Dublin he had never registered, leaving his brother to look after the formalities—but it was never done. It so happened that I knew a Mr Redmond, the aliens officer in charge of immigration to Ireland. He was one of my father's customers and I had met him a few times. I called to see him in his office in Dublin Castle. I said that I wanted to put a hypothetical question to him about someone who lived in Dublin for over forty years. His reply came immediately. 'Do you mean Benny Farbenbloom? We know about Benny. He is a hardworking man and hasn't bothered anybody.'

I explained about the marriage plans and asked what Benny should do now. Mr Redmond asked where he was registered before he came to Ireland. I told him it was in Bow Street in London which was blasted in the air raids. 'Excellent,' said Mr Redmond. 'So there are no records anywhere else. That makes it much easier. No paper work.' He said that Benny should apply for naturalisation and his application would not be opposed. So Benny was at last able to get married and it was a very good marriage and he at last had a home.

At a meeting held in Zion Schools early in 1940, Robert Briscoe TD called on the young men of the community to play an active role in the armed forces. Many joined the Local Defence Force (LDF), the Local Security Force (LSF) or the Air Raid Protection (ARP) service, and some enlisted in the army. Ireland was neutral but the government was determined to be ready if necessary to resist invasion from any quarter.

Six boys immediately said they would join the army. They were Jackie Harrison, Maurice Factor, Sam Danker, Malcolm Glass, Aaron

Fine and Billy Cornick. They were urging me to go with them. I said, 'Listen boys, you are not joining the boy scouts. If you join the army you are in for a number of years. I'm going to join the LDF.' The LDF attracted a large number of Jewish men. We trained regularly and the only difference to being in the army was that we did not live in barracks. When Jackie Harrison was in Portobello Barracks, his mother would bring a cooked chicken for his Friday meal, but the chicken often went missing.

Young Jewish men also served in the British forces during the war. My brother Harry decided to go up to Belfast and join the RAF after he had a row with my eldest brother Sam. He was attached to the maintenance section when, by chance, he met Ivor Green. Ivor had left his father's furniture shop for some reason and had joined the RAF also. He was inclined to be a daredevil and wanted to be a rear gunner which was the most dangerous position in a fighter plane. Harry persuaded Ivor to join the maintenance section instead. Both of them survived the war and returned to their respective jobs.

The first casualty of war that we heard of was William Collins, the caretaker of the Jewish School. Before taking up his job as caretaker he had been a sailor on one of the British warships and was still in the navy reserve. When war was declared he was called up to join the HMS *Courageous*. He left at once and his wife carried on as caretaker of the school. He died when his ship was torpedoed during the Battle of Britain. Binney (Bernard) White was another early casualty. Binney was a neighbour of mine in Victoria Street. He joined the RAF and was shot down in the Battle of Britain. He was a younger brother of Henry White who became a leading manufacturer of women's garments. The business built up by Henry White is still being carried on by his two sons who are leading figures in the fashion trade today.

When the war ended, many more Jews came to live in Ireland. The Elzas family came at this time. Their background was Dutch.

They were strictly orthodox and they became members of the Adelaide Road Synagogue. They started a factory in Leixlip manufacturing parchment and manuscript paper, a business they were in when they were in Holland. They were highly respected by the community, to which they added a spiritual dignity. They lived in Dublin for more than ten years and made a very significant impact.

Mr Safran was another very religious person who came to live here after the war. He married Hetty Steinberg, one of Jack's sisters. Jack Steinberg married Lena Freedman. After Lena's death he married Hennie, the widow of Lenny Herman. Mr Safran joined the Terenure Synagogue where his brother-in-law Jack Steinberg was also a member, and he was regularly present for morning and evening prayers in the *minyan* rooms. Mr Safran started a small factory manufacturing children's anoraks.

After some years, the Safrans and the Steinbergs decided to move to Manchester because of what they considered to be a deterioration in *Yiddishkeit*. Willy Zeider and his wife also left for Manchester for the same reason. It was at this time that the leaders of the community should have begun to take notice of what was happening in their midst. Nobody expressed an opinion as to why the Elzas and the Safrans, and later Jack Steinberg and his wife, decided to leave Dublin and go to Manchester. People were leaving for other reasons also. Shops were closing because children had no interest in taking over businesses that their parents had built up. Some were moving to Israel at a time when people were needed to go and live there. Also there were those who had decided for health reasons to move to a warmer climate.

The community was beginning to be more affluent and the religious atmosphere was beginning to wane. *Kosher* butchers began to close in Clanbrassil Street. Hilda Fine opened her shop in Terenure to cater for people who had moved to that area. She stocked many of the Jewish foods such as home made cheese and *smethena*, chopped liver, herring; also cinnamon strips and cakes baked by her sister Doris. Eventually the years took their toll and Hilda had to close the shop. There was nobody willing to carry it on, and this left only one Jewish shop. This was Beila Erlich's butcher shop. Beila was forced to stock part of her shop with groceries in response to the continuing demand for *kosher* foods and the gradual closing down of so many of the other shops in Clanbrassil Street.

Many of the businesses that parents had worked hard to build up had to close because the children had no desire to carry them on. With regard to manufacturing companies, they had good reason. With the war over, countries that had been involved in the conflict began to export all kinds of goods to Ireland. Most of the factories were not able to compete with these imports, and the children of parents who had started a business had to look for alternative ways to make a living. Some of the furniture manufacturers became involved in the DIY business and also turned to supplying timber of various qualities to the smaller manufacturers and to builders. Many others emigrated in search of new opportunities.

# 13 *Balebatim* and Others

*Balebatim* is a special Yiddish word used to refer to persons of high standing and impeccable reputation, outstanding members of the community. I would select Arthur Newman, Mick Jacobson and Morris Ellis as the three *balebatim* of Dublin. Arthur Newman's son Victor, who is in his ninety-first year, remembers his father telling him how he came to Ireland with his family when he was about five years old. The family and practically the whole village in the Kovno area of Lithuania decided to get away from Russia around 1880. They had experienced anti-Semitic attacks, not unlike those seen in the film *Fiddler on the Roof.* When the ship dropped them off in Cobh (Queenstown at the time) they thought they were in America— which was where they wanted to go. Arthur recalled that the small community in Cork helped them and the other new arrivals with food and accommodation when they arrived.

The family name was Nimina, but it was changed to Newman which was easier to spell and pronounce. When he was old enough to work, Arthur went to Limerick. There he got a job in a drapery shop owned by a Mr Graff. He was paid the sum of £1 per week, which was a great deal of money at that time. The family eventually moved to Dublin and lived in Ovoca Road near Clanbrassil Street. Arthur's father (Victor's grandfather) was a Reverend and a *shochet* and was no doubt able to support the family.

Arthur was a first class tailor and he opened a small factory in Coppinger Row off South William Street, where he made suits for members of the British Army in Dublin. He moved later to larger premises in Abbey Street to manufacture demob clothing, also for the army. His first venture into the retail clothing business was in 1930. Later, Victor was put in charge of the shop in 24 Henry Street, and his brother Ernest had the responsibility of running the other Henry Street shop at No. 6. Later there was another shop in O'Connell Street, and two more in North Earl Street.

Soon after his arrival in Ireland, Arthur Newman began to take an interest in the community, and some time before 1920 he was made a Justice of the Peace. From 1920 to 1923 he served as President of the Adelaide Road Synagogue. He also chaired the committee set up to raise funds to extend the synagogue, providing 123 additional seats for men and sixty additional seats for the women. As he became more involved, his talent as a leader was recognised. He was an ardent Zionist as were many members of the community at that time. He represented Ireland at a meeting of the British Board of Deputies in London and met many Zionist leaders there. He invited Jabotinsky, one of the leaders of the Zionist movement, to address the Jewish community in Dublin in 1938. They met privately at the home of Mick Jacobson along with Effie Seligman to discuss ways and means to raise funds for use in Palestine.

He played an important part in the establishment of Zion Schools. He was involved in discussions with the Minister for Education which resulted in a government grant of £10,000. A site was bought in Bloomfield Avenue just opposite the house that was used by the *Talmud Torah* (Hebrew school). As president of the building committee, Arthur laid the foundation stone on 19 December 1932. The official opening ceremony took place on Sunday 4 March 1934, and the honour of opening the school was given to Morris Ellis with a key presented to him by Arthur Newman. Following numerous speeches introduced by Dr G. Wigoder and toasts proposed by Rabbi Herzog and Reverend Gudansky, a portrait of Arthur Newman was unveiled and presented to him. Then Mrs Baker was presented with a Golden Book certificate in the name of her late husband, Philip

Baker, who was the Hon. Treasurer of the *Talmud Torah*.

In the evening, Arthur Newman presided at a banquet where there were many more toasts, including one to the success of the school and to all who had a part in the building of the school. Glowing references to the President were made by other leaders of the community also, including Dr Leonard Abrahamson, Mr Maslin and Mr Tomkin. Jack Zlotover proposed a special toast in appreciation of the work of the Ladies' Committee. Mrs Sherowitz responded as Hon. President of the *Talmud Torah* Ladies' Committee. The final toast was to Arthur Newman. It was proposed by Bernard Shillman and Herman Good, acknowledging Arthur's unfailing support for a project that was so dear to him, the education of Jewish children. It was a clear recognition of his leadership in the community.

My sister Sadie has reminded me that she attended Hebrew classes three times a week in the new school. Rooms were also available for meetings in the evening. Esther Khan was the secretary of a number of societies, including the Jewish National Fund, and her knowledge of events was unsurpassed. I have often thought that her contribution to the community wasn't sufficiently appreciated.

Early in 1937, when the new Irish Constitution was being formulated, Chief Rabbi Isaac Herzog was one of the religious leaders consulted and Arthur Newman was with him when he went to meet Mr de Valera. When Arthur and his wife celebrated their Golden Wedding, the Taoiseach (Prime Minister) John A. Costello was the honoured guest. His presence on this occasion was an acknowledgement of a lifetime of service for both Jews and non-Jews in Dublin. Arthur Newman died in January 1968 at the age of ninety-four. He was without doubt the most outstanding Jew in Dublin in his day.

Arthur's son Ernest qualified as a solicitor before he was called upon to manage the shop at 6 Henry Street while his brother Victor managed the first shop at 24 Henry Street. Through his involvement in the community, Ernest followed in his father's footsteps. He became president of the Jewish Representative Council, a very onerous position where his knowledge of the law was often helpful in sorting out difficult matters. He was also active in getting the B'Nai B'rith started in Dublin and was one of the early presidents of the society. He and his wife Renée had three children, two boys and a girl. The eldest son, Robert, managed one of the shops in North Earl Street. I knew him through business and found him to be a charming person. Unfortunately, he was drowned in Spain as a result of a tragic accident. The second son, Paul, went into the property market and is now one of the leading auctioneers in the greater Dublin area. Ernest's daughter, Jane, married one of the Esses boys from a family of leading agents in Dublin.

Mick Jacobson came from Riga in 1889. His family name was Aronson. This was changed when he was brought to Dublin by an uncle named Jacobson who lived in Clanbrassil Street, where he sold mineral water. Mick was employed by a decorating company. He trained as a painter and decorator and eventually set up his own company. His wife was one of three sisters who lived in Lancaster in the north of England, having originally come from Austria. One sister married Hyman Shaper's father and another married one of the Samuels family. The third sister worked for her brother-in-law in his jewellery shop in Camden Street until she married Mike Jacobson. Some time later, they also went into the jewellery business and opened their own shop in Lower Camden Street.

During the 1916 rebellion they bought a shop in Henry Street that had been severely damaged in the fighting. With his expertise as a painter and decorator and his knowledge of the building trade, Mick rebuilt the shop. They now had a jewellery shop in one of the best business streets in Dublin. When the Civil War ended they opened another shop in O'Connell Street, a few yards from Clery's. They had three children, Noel, Hilda and Louis.

In the early 1920s Mick became a keen Zionist. He visited Palestine in 1925 and saw for himself the work that was being done to clear the land and drain the swamps. He watched young boys and girls working to make the land fit for the people who were beginning to arrive in large numbers. In 1938 he entertained Jabotinsky in his home, invited a group of people to meet him, and made a commitment to raise money to buy arms which would be used for defensive purposes by the young *kibbutznicks* in Palestine. Seventy-five years later, his son Louis still remembers this gathering. He remembers that Effie Seligman was there but can't recall who the others were.

Mick Jacobson was on the council of the Greenville Hall Synagogue and was one of the planners of the new synagogue that opened in 1925. He also championed sporting activities for youth. When it was realised that the grounds of the Carlisle Club in Parkmore Drive were too small for the community, a large plot of ground was leased from Dublin Corporation and Mick Jacobson and Morris Ellis funded the cost of building the new pavilion. Mick died in 1978. His generosity and wisdom were greatly appreciated and his death was a sad loss to the community.

Morris Ellis presided at the opening of the Greenville Hall Synagogue and guided it through difficult years. I first met him when I was working in my father's factory during the school holidays. I used to be sent to deliver suits to his rooms on the first floor over a shop in Henry Street. He was very meticulous and careful about detail. He would examine every item and if a garment did not come up to his standards he would tell me to bring it back to be altered.

Morris was a down to earth person and had no time for frivolities. If something needed to be done, he made sure that it was done. His wife also played her part on various committees. Few people knew of his generosity to many charities. He added a quality to the community that set a standard not easily reached, and only those who had personal contact with him knew how kind he really was. If

I were asked to name the most prominent members of the community during the 1920s and 1930s, Morris Ellis would be in the first three. His work is carried on in Dublin by his granddaughter Estelle Menton and grandson Alan Miller, children of Sybil and Dr Joe Miller. Their grandparents would be rightfully proud of their involvement in the community. Estelle is the chairwoman of the Representative Council and Alan is president of the Holy Burial Society. Estelle is married to Seton Merton, a well known dentist in Dublin.

The Yiddish word *baleboosteh* means an outstanding woman, and I cannot think of a more outstanding woman in the community than the late Beila Erlich. I got to know the Erlich family when we moved to Victoria Street in the early 1930s. They lived beside the Walworth Road *shul* but Mr Erlich was a member of the Greenville Hall *shul*. He was a butcher and had a shop in Clanbrassil Street. Beila's brother Myer attended the Walworth Road *shul* and I used to meet him there at the Friday night and Saturday services. I remember that he had a very stern grandmother who seemed to be always reprimanding him for something or other. I often saw people going into the Erlichs' house after the Saturday morning service and I knew from this that they were very hospitable.

When I married Riv, I learned that her father was related to Mr Erlich. Their families had come from the same small town in Russia and Beila always considered Riv as her cousin. On *Shevuoth* (the holiday of the first fruits) and *Succoth*, Riv and I and my parents-in-law would visit the Erlichs. The first thing I noticed when we went into their house was the table laden with homemade delicacies, prepared no doubt by their daughter Rose who was well known for her cooking. Rose worked as a secretary for Harry Singer. Sadly, she became ill and had to go into Jervis Street Hospital. The diagnosis was cancer. Riv went to see her in hospital nearly every day, until she died at a very young age.

Beila, when she left school, went to help her father in the butcher's shop. When Mr Erlich died in 1971 she took over responsibility for managing the shop herself. But she had some good friends, and none better than Harry and Hymie Woolfson who helped her to move to a better position in Clanbrassil Street. It was they who arranged for her to purchase the premises still known by everyone as Erlich's. Beila did not have a great deal of schooling. No doubt, she had to leave school at an early age to help at home, but she had a flair for figures and a brain like a calculator. She also had a sharp tongue that she would not hesitate to use with difficult customers, and she was able to talk to any of her meat suppliers in a language they understood.

She had a deep concern for old people, and many who lived alone at that time would testify to her kindness. Parcels of food provided by her were regularly brought to them by her brother Myer. Myer was kind and generous but was not much help in the shop. Beila was very glad when he took over the *shul* in the Jewish Home. He had a rich baritone voice and was more than capable of leading the service on Friday night, on Saturday and on the Festivals.

In the late 1970s, Beila decided to move to Terenure with her brother Myer and Lena Green, her housekeeper and companion. When she heard that Nat Mendel was leaving Dublin and selling his house in Wasdale Park, she asked Riv to go with her to talk to him. When it came to agreeing a price Riv took over the negotiations, prompting Nat to ask who was buying the house. A deal was done and Beila moved in with the help of a lot of her friends. The back garden of the house overlooked the grounds of Terenure Synagogue and Nat Mendel, who was at one time President, had put a door in the wall to provide a short cut to the *shul*. Beila decided to leave the door, and from then on there was a steady flow of people walking through her house or the side passage if it was open. Going around by the Terenure Road from Wasdale Park took ten minutes longer. Beila loved to have people in her house and it was open for them to come to her for *Kiddush* after *shul* and even stay for lunch.

With the closing down of so many grocery and butcher shops that had catered for the community, Erlich's became the only *kosher* butcher shop left in Clanbrassil Street. Beila had a loyal staff but she was the person who had to deal with suppliers of meat, chickens and turkeys. They had great respect for her integrity. She was forever on the phone to the cross-channel suppliers of grocery items. The shop was always stocked with a wide variety of goods, including wine. She had two large freezers in the passage of her home filled to capacity, and she also had a large fridge-freezer in her kitchen. The shop had to undergo a face-lift to hold all the items she was carrying.

She had two non-Jewish women cooking foodstuffs in her home for sale in the shop. They made chopped liver and herrings, and *perogen* that were very popular with her customers. These women were very loyal to Beila and completely trustworthy, and I am sure they were well rewarded. They had worked for her for years and knew everything about *kashrut*. Beila quite often questioned a point of *kashrut* with the Rabbi when he visited the shop. She would not accept the Rabbi's or anyone else's opinion regarding *kashrut* if she thought they were wrong. And in most cases she was right. Of course, she had helpers at all times. Helen Green who had worked for Hilda Fine was a wonderful support. But it was remarkable that this one person, Beila Erlich, should be responsible for feeding the community.

There were two non-Jewish butchers working in the shop. Paul had been in Erlich's for over fifty years when Beila died in 1998. Over the years he had acquired a smattering of Yiddish expressions. Dominick, who is still working in the shop, has been there for fourteen years along with Alec Goldwater. Alec comes from a family of butchers who were in Clanbrassil Street. His father, Isaac, was a very colourful character and was always ready for a chat. I remember him as a very generous and obliging man. He was typical of his generation that came to Dublin from Russia. They were hard-working men whose wives often helped them in the shop as well as rearing children and running a home.

For many years I conducted the two *Seder* nights in Beila's house. Myer was content for me to do this. It enabled him to rest, as he would be reciting the morning prayers in the Home. We had some very enjoyable *Seders* with twelve or more people present. Beila had very efficient helpers. One of these was Freda Jacks who lived alone in St Kevin's Parade. She was like a sister to Beila for many years and would be staying overnight at festivals or over the *Shabbos*. There was also Laila Kronn who lived across the road from Beila and became very friendly with her after she came to live in Wasdale Park

Beila had an open house on Saturday afternoons and many people (mainly women) called in for tea, bringing or hearing news of events in the community. I myself often accompanied Riv. She would go upstairs to talk to Beila, who would be resting in bed. Even though she could have many visitors, she would come downstairs later. Her close friend, Freda Jacks, would make the tea. When Beila died, it changed the habits of quite a number of people.

When she became ill, her friend Dr Kenny Harris looked after her. He tried to get her to ease up and take more rest, but to no avail. She felt that she had a responsibility to the community and carried on until she was forced to go into hospital, to St Vincent's. Riv and I and some other friends were there, and we waited until she settled in. She would not eat anything cooked in the hospital, so her butcher Paul came in every day with hot meals cooked for her by her friends. She was in a small four-bed ward, and the other patients looked on in amazement when they saw the different containers arriving. She would not even drink juices or water from utensils belonging to the hospital.

One day when we were visiting her we heard her on the phone in the ward, giving instructions from her bed regarding the order for *Pesach* and telling the supplier in England in no uncertain terms when she expected the goods to be delivered. The nurses were really wonderful and responded to her many demands that were mainly to do with the shop and supplies for the shop. What stories the other patients could tell their families and friends about this small woman who had had an endless stream of visitors including the Chief Rabbi and Cantor Shulman.

After several weeks in hospital, Beila was able to return to her own house and Kenny Harris continued to keep a close watch on her condition. She paid a few visits to the shop, but she tired quickly and was glad when Paul took her home. Gradually, she began to improve. As *Pesach* was approaching, she arranged to have the *Pesach* foods sold from her house and had no trouble getting volunteers to help. She herself would go to the shop where she also had supplies. When she decided to have the *Seder* at her house her friends tried in vain to talk her out of it. She had made her mind up. She must have thought that it might be the last one. Her friends rallied around and we made it a very enjoyable occasion. I am happy that I officiated at what was to be the last *Seder* at Beila's house.

At *Simchath Torah*, the final day of *Succoth*, I used to go to the Jewish Home where Beila always provided goodies for the festival. When she could no longer walk there, a number of young boys borrowed a wheelchair and called to her house to bring her to the Home. Her health continued to deteriorate and she was again admitted to St Vincent's Hospital where she died on 8 August 1998. Her funeral was one of the largest ever to take place in Dublin. In my opinion, Beila Erlich was the best known and most loved person in the entire Jewish community and Dublin will never be the same without her.

One *Shabbos* in 1981, when I was in Adelaide Road *shul*, I was told that Louis Steinberg was in the Meath Hospital and was very ill. In fact I was told that he had cancer. Our family was very friendly with the Steinbergs. My brother Harry and I used to go to their home on South Circular Road on *Pesach* after we had finished our *Seder*, and Louis Steinberg played an important role at the time of our father's remarriage. He had worked for my father when the family came to Dublin from Czechoslovakia at the end of the 1920s. He was a brother of Ettie Steinberg who died in the Holocaust. He was a close friend of my brother Hymie. He was an active member of the community, and gave great service to the Holy Burial Society of Dublin for many years along with his father.

I decided to visit him in hospital, because I knew that none of the family would be visiting him on *Shabbos*. It was too far for them to walk, so they would not be there until later in the day when *Shabbos* was out, or possibly not until the next day. I went to the hospital from *shul* as it was quite near. I enquired what room Louis was in. I knocked on the door and went in. I saw Louis standing at the window with his *talith* draped around his shoulders, deep in prayer. He looked up and saw me. His eyes filled with tears as he grasped my hand and said 'How wonderful to see a Yiddish face today when I wasn't expecting anyone.' I stayed with him for some time and was reluctant to leave.

When I arrived home, I told Riv where I had been and said I found it hard to believe that he had cancer. I went to see Louis on two more occasions and then I heard that he was being moved to St Luke's cancer hospital. When I visited him in St Luke's I noticed a dramatic change in his appearance and he was semi-conscious. He died in April 1981. When I went to the *shivah* house, his wife Myra and his son David thanked me for the *mitzvah* (kind deed) I did in visiting the hospital on *Shabbos*.

One of the most popular members of the community was Bob Lepler, one of the group that formed the Jewish Dramatic Society. He was an ebullient character with an engaging smile and exuberant personality. Other members of the JDS were Dora Coleman, Dahna Davis, Gladys Spain, Harry Moscow, Cleo and Joe Morrison, Sydney

Lanarus and Raphael Seligman. Some of the plays were performed in the Abbey Theatre and others later in the Gaiety.

In 1937 Bob was invited by Lord Longford to join his company, and he went with them for a season in Westminster Theatre in London. Later he performed in plays put on by Hilton Edwards and Micheál Mac Liammóir, one being *Arsenic and Old Lace* which gave him the utmost pleasure as he took the part of the Jewish doctor, and because he played with Liam Gaffney, the well-known actor.

Bob continued his involvement in acting, but also found time to put on plays himself. He also put on the musical *The Mikado*, in which he played the part of the Lord High Executioner, Dave Maslin was Nanky Poo and Leila Eppel was Yum Yum. This musical was held in the Town Hall, Rathmines for two nights. I took part as one of the chorus.

In 1962 Bob was interviewed for *Chadashot,* a Dublin Jewish weekly newsletter, on his views on the community, and the fact that the Jewish Dramatic Society no longer functioned. He was scathing about the Dublin Jewry, describing them as apathetic, saying that it was outrageous that with so much talent around there was no longer a Jewish Dramatic Society.

Other interests of Bob's were shared with Louis Hyman, author of *The Jews of Ireland*. They formed the Habonim, a movement intended to help train the youth in farming and ultimately to go to Israel. Bob was also the representative of the Federation of Zionist Youth.

One of the best known Jewish artists in Dublin was Harry Kernoff, who was born in London in 1900, but came to Dublin in 1914 with his parents and other members of the family. They lived in Stamer Street, off the South Circular Road. From an early age he had a love for painting and attended night classes at the Metropolitan School of Art. His work was mainly on Irish subjects, and he won the Taylor Art Scholarship in 1923.

He became involved in the theatre, and designed and made sets for Micheál Mac Liammóir and Hilton Edwards, and for W. B. Yeats. He was the business manager of the Gate Theatre in 1929,when Larry Elyan took part in the well known Irish play *The Shadow of a Gunman,* which portrayed life in Dublin during the Troubles.In 1935, he was honoured by being elected as a member of the Royal Hibernian Academy. Most of his paintings were produced between the years 1940 and 1945. Unfortunately, during his lifetime he never achieved the popularity of other artists, and he was often reduced to selling his paintings for very little money. He was helped out by many of his friends. He died in December 1974. Today his paintings are in great demand and selling at prices he never would have dreamed of.

Estella Solomons, another famous artist, was born in Dublin in 1882 and learned her craft in Dublin and Hanover. In Dublin she studied in the Metropolitan School of Art under the tuition of such esteemed artists as William Orpen and Walter Osborne. She rarely exhibited her work, but her portraits were well known and appeared at annual exhibitions of the Royal Hibernian Academy. She was also elected as an Honorary Academician in 1966. She died in Dublin in 1968.

Gerald Davis is a very popular member of the community. He studied painting at the National College of Art. His first exhibition took place in 1962 in Dublin and since then he has exhibited in other places in Ireland and internationally, including in major Irish group exhibitions, such as the Royal Hibernian Academy during the 1960s and 70s. Many of his paintings are in private and public collections in Ireland and overseas. He opened his gallery in Capel Street in 1970. In 1977 he was awarded the Douglas Hyde Gold Medal.

The first Jewish members of the community to enter the Civil Service were the two Eliasoff brothers who lived on the South Circular

Road in 1922. I can clearly remember the two of them walking from their home  to Dublin Castle where they worked, and whenever their name comes up I am reminded of an incident that occurred in the Jewish Museum in 1999.

I was on duty with a colleague and a man came in with a box in his hands. He said he was not Jewish, but he had just moved into a house on the South Circular Road, and had found the box in his attic. He said it contained honours certificates won by people with names he recognised as Jewish. We thanked him and looked through the contents of the box. There were quite a number of certificates that had been awarded to two members of the family who had lived in that house, and the names on the certificates were those of the two Eliasoff brothers.

About an hour later a young woman came into the Museum and I asked her to sign the visitors' book and, as a matter of curiosity, asked her where she came from. She told me she came from Geneva. She was looking for information about a grandfather or great-grandfather of hers who had lived in Dublin, and when I asked her the name of this person, she replied (yes, you've guessed it), Eliasoff. Needless to say she was delighted when we produced the box so she could take notes of her family.

Raphael Siev, curator of the Museum, entered the Civil Service in 1968. His first posting was with the Department of Justice and in 1970 he was transferred to the Department of Foreign Affairs, where he served with distinction until he retired in September 2000.

Max Factor is another person who joined the Civil Service in 1977. He started in the Fisheries and Forest Department and then moved to the Office of Public Works. Max is still in the Service.

Larry Elyan, who came from Cork to live in Dublin, went to work in the Civil Service in the 1920s. His brother Victor also came to live in Dublin and qualified as a solicitor and went into practice with Raphael Seligman and Barney Bernstein in rooms in Dame

Street.

However, Larry Elyan was always in the centre of activities, whether it was for charity or taking part in debates. He joined the Progressive Synagogue when it opened in 1946 and played a great part in its establishment.

While in Dublin he was a member of the Jewish Dramatic Society. He also took part in plays produced by Hilton Edwards in the Gate Theatre as an amateur. His talents were rewarded when he was given the part of the Bishop in Bernard Shaw's play *St Joan* with the renowned Irish actress Siobhan McKenna, also at the Gate Theatre.

When Israel was declared a state in 1948, Larry decided to leave Dublin to assist the future of Israel in some way, and he took part in Israel's radio programmes. He went on the overseas programme and read the news in English. He died in Israel.

Another Jewish person who was in the Civil Service at the same time as Larry Elyan was Robby Khan. The family came under a lot of attention during the Troubles in Dublin. As a group of Jewish men were coming out of the Literary Club in Harrington Street, including Robby Khan, his brother and a few more people, shooting was heard and Robby Khan's brother was shot dead.

Nobody was sure if the group were the actual target, but the fact was that an innocent man was killed. An inquiry was set up by the police. Robby Khan himself made inquiries and it was said he had traced the person who was thought to have fired the fatal shot to a street off Palmerston Road, only to find that he had fled to England, and there the matter ended.

Robby Khan had another position besides being a Civil Servant; he was the *Jewish Chronicle*'s representative in Dublin until he died in 1952. His sister Esther continued her late brother's position until 1979 when she became ill and was admitted to the Jewish Home from Ovoca Road, off the South Circular Road, where she had lived.

I knew Esther personally. She was never married. She was small in stature, but was full of energy. She had an office in the Zion schools and many times I went to see her about some matter relating to the Jewish National Fund of which she was the secretary. She seldom smiled but was extremely efficient in her work. She was responsible for a calendar being set up to prevent different events clashing with each other in the community.

We got on very well so long as I did not contradict her in her work. She also played a big part when the B'Nai Brith was started in Dublin. I can recall her speaking on the phone to someone in the B'Nai Brith in London, and her caustic remarks as to their efficiency. At the time I was secretary of the B'Nai Brith.

Esther was the perfect secretary, she had everything at her fingertips. To my mind she was never rewarded for the part she played on behalf of the Jewish community. She was a real treasure.

Elaine Freeman was the first Jewish woman to enter the Civil Service during the 1930s. She was there for some years and married Jack Feldman. Unfortunately at that period, when a woman married she had to leave her job. The same applied to nurses. This was no doubt due to the acute unemployment situation at the time.

Other members of the community who have recently entered the Civil Service are Edwin Alkin and Jane Barron, daughter of the former High Court Judge Henry Barron, now the Chairman of the Irish Jewish Museun. Both are in the Attorney General's office in Dublin.

I got to know Harry Singer in the 1930s. He came from Manchester and arrived in Dublin as a very young man, some time before 1930. He found a home with the Erlich family in Walworth Road. He was a sewing machine mechanic and he rented a shop at the Liffey Street end of Abbey Street. He repaired and sold second-hand sewing machines. He also serviced Hoffman pressing machines. I remember that he had a pressing machine set up in his premises.

He was a workaholic and spent most of his time rebuilding the second-hand sewing machines that he had bought. Gradually, he built up the business and in time was selling new machinery. He did all the work himself with the help of Rose Erlich, a daughter of the family he was living with. She looked after the books and dealt with any enquiries when Harry was out.

One day Harry wanted to have his only suit pressed for some function to which he was invited. He found that none of the cleaners such as Imco or Prescotts would undertake just to press a suit. They would of course clean the suit and then press it, but they definitely would not press it without having it cleaned. So, Harry pressed the suit himself on the pressing machine that he had in his own premises.

While he was pressing the suit, it occurred to him that if he could not find anybody to press his suit, there must be hundreds of people in the same boat. He took another shop just beside the *Independent* newspaper offices and set up two pressing machines for the sole purpose of pressing men's suits and ladies' costumes. The business took off immediately and he gave up selling and repairing sewing machines to devote his time to this new undertaking.

He then began to take an interest in dry cleaning. He decided to go to America where he had a relative in the dry cleaning business, so as to get a full knowledge of the process. When he returned from the States, he set up a dry cleaning plant that he had purchased there. He carried out all the work himself and soon opened for business under the name of the New York Cleaning Company. Just before World War II he had a telephone call from his mother in Manchester, asking if he would give his younger brother Myer a job in his business. His immediate response was 'Let him come over at once. What I have, he will share.'

The business prospered as Harry and now Myer devoted their time to looking after it, keeping a watchful eye on everything and often making a spot check to be sure that a garment was properly cleaned. Unfortunately, Harry's health began to deteriorate and the headaches from which he had suffered for some time got worse. He died at the age of forty-four, and it was so sad that he didn't live to enjoy the fruits of his labour. The business continued in the capable hands of Myer who never married, and it is now being carried by his niece Fay Milofsky and one of her sons.

Morry Gordon arrived from Chicago in 1932. His uncle Abraham Bellow was in business in Leeds, where he manufactured sewing machines and other appliances related to the clothing trade. He came over to Dublin and helped his nephew to set up a branch to sell Bogod sewing machines produced in his factory in Leeds. At that time the Singer Sewing Machine Company had a monopoly on the business in Ireland. Morry, as he became known, set about visiting the many Jewish-owned clothing factories. Because of his attractive personality and because he was offering a good product he began to create openings for the sale of Bogod machines. I can remember my father giving Morry an order, and many of the other clothing factories did likewise.

His first premises were in Liffey Street. As the business developed he moved to Upper Abbey Street, to Capel Street, and then to much larger premises in Mary's Abbey just off Capel Street. Eventually he moved to Inchicore, where he consolidated his operations and was very helpful to people who were starting up in business. He was there to advise them as to their needs and allowed them credit for long periods. I know this, because I was one of those people when I got married and decided to set up my own business in 1942. He traded under the name Machines Ltd, and he equipped my factory in Pleasants Place with machines and pressing plant without ever asking for immediate payment.

Machines Ltd offered serious competition to the Singer Sewing Machine Company and often gave better service. Branches were opened in Cork and in Northern Ireland. Then, World War II ended and Germany began to rebuild its industries. Pfaff sewing machines became available, and in my opinion they were better than those manufactured by either Bogod or Singer. Gradually I began to equip my factory with Pfaff machines, except for some fancy ones that were manufactured in America. This changeover helped to increase my production of men's and youth's slacks. All my machines were supplied by Machines Ltd, who were the Irish agents for the Pfaff machines.

Morry began to involve himself more and more in the Jewish community and it wasn't long before he became a member of the council in the Adelaide Road Synagogue. He also found time to help non-Jewish sports organisations, and he became involved in the Scouts movement. He coached the Irish basketball team for the 1948 Olympics in London, and proudly led the team when they paraded around the stadium. He was elected a member of the Olympic Council of Ireland. He was an excellent swimmer and had been a lifeguard in Chicago before coming to Ireland. He dived from the Ha'penny Bridge to save the life of a young woman who had fallen into the Liffey. In recognition of his bravery he received the Silver Cross, the highest award given by the Irish Boy Scouts. When he retired from the Scouts he received the Silver Elk award. He had the distinction of being the longest serving Jewish scout in the world.

Morry married Rae Gross, who grew up in the Curragh, Co. Kildare. Her family was very orthodox and had decided to come to Dublin to live. Morry and Rae had three children. The eldest, Lawrence, qualified as a dentist and emigrated to New York where he set up in practice. Adrian went into his father's business at an early age, and like his father he took a great interest in community affairs. His wife Marise played an important part in teaching Hebrew Education and Jewish Studies in Stratford College. The third son, Niall (or Dick as he was more popularly known) was also in the business for some years until he and his Dublin-born wife Meriel moved to Canada, where Meriel's mother Gladys Spain also lives.

When Morry Gordon died on 21 May 1990 his coffin was brought to Adelaide Road Synagogue, where he had given over fifty years of service and had been President from 1978 to 1981. Rabbi Mirvis gave a eulogy in which he referred to Morry Gordon's efforts to promote harmony in the community, and to his contribution to Jewish and non-Jewish organisations. Among those who came to pay their respects were the internationally-known pianist John O'Conor, Richard Tennant, the head of the Scouting Association of Ireland, and representatives of the Olympic Council of Ireland. Morry Gordon's funeral was one of the largest funerals in the history of the Dublin Jewish community and I, for one, was proud to be a friend of his.

When the subject of the most prominent leaders in the Dublin Jewish community comes up, I always think of Hubert Wine. When Herman Good died in 1981 after many years as leader of the community and Life President of the Adelaide *shul*, Hubert stepped into his place as his natural successor. Hubert is the son of Harry Wine, who was probably the best-known antiques dealer in Ireland. Harry Wine was also well known in England and in New York, and was always happy to advise any young people who were hoping to make a career in the antiques business.

Following family tradition Hubert had devoted much time to the Adelaide Road Synagogue, having served as Council member and Warden for many years. He also served the community through his work on a number of committees and he had a deep knowledge of the *chumash* (the five Books of Moses). He was the obvious choice for the position of Life President when Herman Good died.

When Hubert Wine qualified as a solicitor he worked in the firm of Herman Good & Co. before setting up his own practice. In due course he was appointed a Judge of the District Court. His name became prominent in newspaper reports of court cases, because he often criticised the government's failure to provide more suitable accommodation for young boys and girls than Mountjoy Prison where they would have to mix with hardened criminals. Hubert has now retired from the Bench, but he continues to play an important part in the community. I hope he can do so for many more years, as there are very few people who could take his place.

Personally, I cannot see anyone who would even want to take on the very serious problems that have arisen in the Jewish community. The only shop that sold *kosher* food has closed. Since Adelaide Road Synagogue closed members of the Council have reached no decision about what kind of *shul* is needed. It seems to me that there is a lack of harmony between the Council of the Adelaide Road Synagogue and the Council of the Terenure Synagogue. We need leadership very badly. We need someone who is respected by the community and who is able to show the various sections of the people how to survive as a community.

Dublin Jewry has reached a low ebb compared to the days when we had a thriving community. Some of the older members are concerned by the fact that young people are leaving. They suggest inviting Jewish families living in South Africa to move to Dublin. Their efforts deserve our encouragement but we need to ask some questions: What can we offer to these same people? Would they want to come to a country with such a high cost of living and where the cost of housing to buy or rent is exorbitant? We don't even have— and in fact have never had—a *kosher* restaurant. There are no sporting activities for Jewish children. We no longer have the cultural activities in which Dublin excelled. And the climate!

One of the older members of the community asked a South African, who is working for a company based in Dublin, if he would bring his wife and family to live here. His reply echoed the objections that I have outlined. He said that a large number of South Africans are thinking of emigrating and he named the countries they had in mind. None of them mentioned Ireland.

If I were asked to predict what the Jewish community in Ireland would be like in fifty years' time I would reply without too much hesitation. I think the community will continue to dwindle in the years ahead, but there will always be an Orthodox Jewish presence here. I would also predict that the Progressive congregation will increase in number, because they accept couples when one of them is Jewish and one (generally the wife) is studying for conversion and wants the children to be Jewish.

# Glossary

*Aliya* — a prayer from the Torah.
*Bagel* — bread roll.
*Balebatim* — outstanding member of the community.
*Baleboosteh* — outstanding woman in the community.
*Bar Mitzvah* — ceremony held on the Saturday nearest to a boy's thirteenth birthday.
*Bat Mitzva* — ceremony for girls when they reach the age of twelve.
*Bema* — central platform in a synagogue.
*Bubba* — grandmother.
*Challa* — braided loaf of bread for the Sabbath.
*Chanukah* — the Feast of Lights.
*Chazan* — Cantor.
*Cheder* — Hebrew school.
*Chevra Kaddishah* — Holy Burial Society.
*Cholent* — a traditional stew-like dish.
*Chomatz* — anything that is not *kosher* for Passover.
*Chumash* — the five Books of Moses.
*Chuppa* — wedding canopy; the word is also used to refer to the wedding ceremony.
*Davening* — praying.
*Dayan* — Rabbi.
*Dradles* — rattles.
*Drosha* — sermon.
*Ehtrog* — citrus fruit, part of the *Succoth* ceremony.
*Frum* — Orthodox.
*Gabbai* — Burial Society contact person.
*Get* — divorce.
*Goy* — non-Jew.
*Haftorah* — a passage from the Prophets, the last part of the reading of the *Torah*.

*Haggadah* — narrative read aloud at the Passover *Seder*.
*Hamantashen* — cakes.
*Heim* — home.
*Inhora* — evil eye.
*Ivrith* — Hebrew spoken in contemporary Israel
*Kaddish* — mourner's prayer.
*Kashrut* — strict observance of *kosher* laws.
*Ketubah* — marriage vows.
*Keiz* — cheese.
*Kiddush* — prayer that sanctifies the Sabbath.
*Kinder* — children.
*Kosher* — in accordance with Jewish dietary laws.
*Kreplach* — a triangular or square dumpling filled with chopped
    meat or cheese.
*Layned* — read.
*Leshana tova* — Happy New Year.
*Lockshen* — noodles, vermicelli.
*Lulav* — palm leaves, part of the *Succoth* ceremony.
*Matzo* — unleavened bread.
*Megillah* — the story of Esther.
*Meshugge* — mad, crazy.
*Mikvah* — ritual bath.
*Mincha* — late-afternoon service.
*Minyan* — ten male Jews required for a religious service.
*Mitzvah* — kind deed.
*Mohel* — circumsiser.
*Musaph* — last part of the *Shabbos* service.
*Nigin* — note of music.
*Pareveh* — made without milk solids or butter fat.
*Perogen* — minced meat rolls.
*Pesach* — Passover.
*Purim* — commemorates the rescue of the Jews from Haman's
    plot to kill them.
*Rosh Hashanah* — Jewish New Year.
*Schmaltz* — cooking fat.
*Seder* — special family gathering at Passover.
*Sedra* — portion of the law in the five books of Moses.
*Sefer Torah* — scroll containing the five books of Moses.

*Shabbos* — Sabbath.

*Shevuoth* — festival of the first fruits.

*Shiddach* — match or marriage.

*Shiur* — a religious discussion

*Shivah* — seven days of solemn mourning.

*Shlogn kapores* — a special ceremony held on the morning before the  fast of *Yom Kippur.*

*Shochet* — authorised slaughterer of animals according to *kosher* requirements.

*Shul* — synagogue.

*Siddur* — prayer book used every day and also on the Sabbath.

*Simchath Torah* — observed on the final day of *Succoth.*

*Smethena* — a type of cheese.

*Succah* — booth used at *Succoth.*

*Succoth* — harvest festival, Feast of Booths (or Tabernacles).

*Talith* — prayer shawl.

*Talmud Torah* — Hebrew school.

*Tefillin* — phylacteries: two thin leather straps, each with a small leather box containing tiny parchments with Hebrew scripture; worn by Orthodox men at morning prayers.

*Tillem* — Book of Proverbs.

*Torah* — the five books of Moses.

*Trayf* — not conforming to Jewish standards.

*Trops* — notes of music.

*Wurst* — sausage.

*Yahrzeit* — prayers on the anniversary of a death.

*Yeshiva* — school for potential Rabbis.

*Yiddishkeit* — religious orthodoxy.

*Yom Kippur* — Day of Atonement, the holiest day of the year.

*Yom Tov* — celebration.

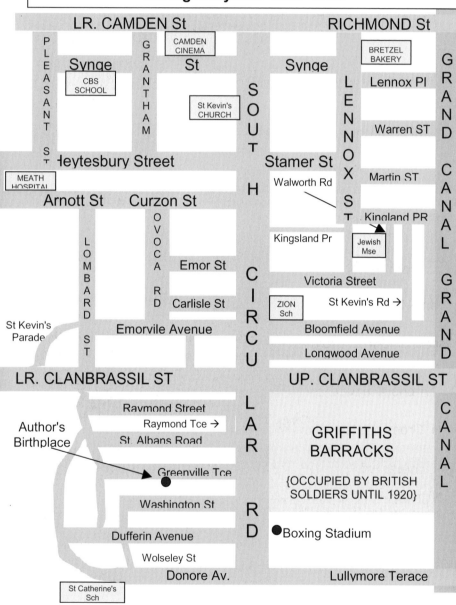

# Where 90 per cent of Jewish community in Dublin lived during the years 1900–1930

LR. CAMDEN St

RICHMOND St

PLEASANT ST

Synge

GRANTHAM

CAMDEN CINEMA

St

Synge

BRETZEL BAKERY

GRAND CANAL

CBS SCHOOL

St Kevin's CHURCH

Lennox Pl

LENNOX ST

Warren ST

SOUTH

Heytesbury Street

Stamer St

Martin ST

MEATH HOSPITAL

Arnott St

Curzon St

Walworth Rd

H

Kingland PR

OVOCA RD

Emor St

Kingsland Pr

Jewish Mse

LOMBARD ST

Carlisle St

ZION Sch

St Kevin's Rd →

St Kevin's Parade

Emorvile Avenue

Victoria Street

Bloomfield Avenue

CIRCULAR

Longwood Avenue

LR. CLANBRASSIL ST

UP. CLANBRASSIL ST

Raymond Street

Raymond Tce →

Author's Birthplace

St. Albans Road

Greenville Tce

GRIFFITHS BARRACKS

{OCCUPIED BY BRITISH SOLDIERS UNTIL 1920}

Washington St

RD

Dufferin Avenue

Boxing Stadium

Wolseley St

Donore Av.

Lullymore Terace

St Catherine's Sch

CANAL

# Shops in Clanbrassil Street, 1930s

Cristol (Photographer)

Goldberg (Bakery)

St Kevin's Parade

Synagogue

**Patrick Street**

Smullen (Milk)

Baigels (Wine)

Myer Rubenstein (Butcher)

Lombard St

Synagogue

Atkins (Bootmaker)

Ordman (Grocer)

Woolf (Drapery)

Erlich (Butcher)

Barrons (Delicatessen)

Philly Rubenstein (Butcher)

M Freedman (Grocer)

Betty Fine (Drapery)

Jackson (Grocer)

Leopold (Poultry)

**Lower Clan-Brassil Street.**

Fine (Milk & Grocer)

Rosedale Terrace

Janie Goldwater Poultry)

Weinrock (Bakery)

A. Samuels (Butcher)

Isaac Goldwater (Butcher)

B. Wertzberger (Wine),

Ab Robinson
{Bookie}

Barrons
(Butcher)

Aronovitch (Grocer)

St. Vincent Street

Hen's Slaughter Hse

H. Gross (Watchmaker)

B. Citron (Butcher)

Newman (Grocer)

5th Circular Rd

***Leonard's Corner***

Sth Circular Rd

Nightingale (Chemist)—
used by Jewish People

**Upper Clan-Brassil Street**

Misstear (Chemist)—
used by Jewish People

Fire Alarm that was
used by Joe Edelstein
to call Fire Brigade

# Index